Contours of Christian Philosophy
C. STEPHEN EVANS *Series Editor*

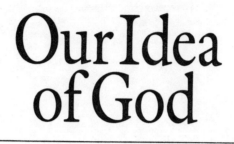

Our Idea of God

An Introduction to Philosophical Theology

Thomas V. Morris

INTERVARSITY PRESS
DOWNERS GROVE, ILLINOIS 60515

InterVarsity Press is the book-publishing division of InterVarsity Christian Fellowship, a student movement active on campus at hundreds of universities, colleges and schools of nursing in the United States of America, and a member movement of the International Fellowship of Evangelical Students. For information about local and regional activities, write Public Relations Dept., InterVarsity Christian Fellowship, 6400 Schroeder Rd., P.O. Box 7895, Madison, WI 53707-7895.

ISBN 0-87784-346-5

Printed in the United States of America ∞

Library of Congress Cataloging-in-Publication Data

Morris, Thomas V.
  Our idea of God: an introduction to philosophical theology/
Thomas V. Morris.
    p.   cm.—(Contours of Christian philosophy)
    Includes bibliographical references.
    ISBN 0-87784-346-5
    1. Philosophical theology.   2. God—Attributes.   I. Title.
II. Series.
BT40.M694   1991
231'.044—dc20   90-19145
                                                        CIP

15	14	13	12	11	10	9	8	7	6	5	4	3	2	1
03	02	01	00	99	98	97	96	95	94	93	92	91		

To Paul and Marcia Bennett,
whose friendship, encouragement
and generosity have enriched
this life in many ways, for
me and for my family.

General Preface

The Contours of Christian Philosophy series will consist of short introductory-level textbooks in the various fields of philosophy. These books will introduce readers to major problems and alternative ways of dealing with those problems. These books, however, will differ from most in that they will evaluate alternative viewpoints not only with regard to their general strength, but also with regard to their value in the construction of a Christian world and life view. Thus, the books will explore the implications of the various views for Christian theology as well as the implications that Christian convictions might have for the philosophical issues discussed. It is crucial that Christians attain a greater degree of philosophical awareness in order to improve the quality of general scholarship and evangelical theology. My hope is that this series will contribute to that end.

Although the books are intended as examples of Christian scholarship, it is hoped that they will be of value to others as well; these issues should concern all thoughtful persons. The assumption which underlies this hope is that complete neutrality in philosophy is neither possible nor desirable. Philosophical work always reflects a person's deepest commitments. Such commitments, however, do not preclude a genuine striving for critical honesty.

C. Stephen Evans
Series Editor

Introduction

Many people, even within the ranks of devout religious believers, have only the haziest conception of God. When this is brought to their attention, a significant number of such people admit that this vagueness about God bothers them deeply, but they often add that they don't have a clue as to how to go about getting clearer on this most important idea. It is one aim of the present book to assist in dealing with this problem. I attempt to provide an example of how some simple, straightforward philosophical methods of thinking can shed light on theological matters which might otherwise remain obscure. It is my hope that this little book will help to stimulate its readers to think more deeply about matters of religious conviction.

This book is also meant to serve as an elementary introduction to philosophical theology. The philosophical issues which can arise concerning so exalted a subject matter as the concept of God can become very complex, and recent treatments of these issues by philosophers have been as technical and demanding as pioneering work in any other field of serious human intellectual inquiry. I have sought to keep my discussions of these issues as streamlined, and as accessible to non-philosophers, as possible. The topic is too important to be reserved for specialists only. In every chapter, I have tried to focus on the most basic issues and to keep complications to a minimum. There are many more technical treatises available for those readers who want to pursue these topics further. My aim is to provide a place to begin.

In these pages, I attempt to focus on some purely conceptual issues. My center of attention is how we think about, or conceive of, God. Hence, the book's title. In another book, I shall be concentrating on questions concerning the rationality of religious belief, the nature of faith, and the cogency of arguments for the existence of God. Those topics are not at the center of my attention here, but the issues which are treated in the present book will be found to hook up with those other topics in numerous and interesting ways. Clarifying our idea of God will put us into a position to make more progress on at least some of these other philosophically important questions.

I want to thank all these friends and colleagues who suggested, and even sometimes insisted over a period of years, that I write such a book. I hope that they are at least to some degree satisfied with the result. I also want to thank all my colleagues who urged that, before beginning the project, I should upgrade my word-processing capability. Everything I have written earlier has been put to paper with a cheap ball-point pen. I decided to take this good advice, and I am happy to acknowledge that the writing of this manuscript was a much more pleasant experience because of my new Pelikan 800 fountain pen, which I enjoyed using throughout. Sherry Reichold, Nancy Kegler, and Cheryl Reed did an excellent job of putting it into a real word processor. Their efforts and results are appreciated.

I also thank everyone who read an earlier version of this book and provided helpful comments. Some parts of the book were scrutinized in the weekly discussion group sponsored by Notre Dame's Center for the Philosophy of Religion. I thank my colleagues in that group for their many pieces of helpful advice. I also want to acknowledge the stimulus provided by written comments sent to me by Stephen Evans, Charles Taliaferro, Jonathan Kvanvig, Jerry Walls and James Sadowski. Portions of chapter nine are drawn from "The Metaphysics of God Incarnate," which has appeared in the book *Trinity, Incarnation and Atonement,* edited by Ronald J. Feenstra and Cornelius Plantinga, Jr. (Notre Dame, Ind.: University of Notre Dame Press, 1989). I thank the editors and Notre Dame Press for the permission to make further use of some of this material. So many facets of our idea of God need to be re-thought again and again because of the inexhaustible resources of this ultimate concept.

Finally, I would like to thank the George A. and Eliza Gardner Howard Foundation for their generous award of a Howard Foundation Fellowship, administered by Brown University, to cover the academic year 1989-90, during which time this project was completed and many others were begun. Time to think is a rare commodity, and a wonderful gift.

1

The Project
of Philosophical
Theology

*T*heology, according to the ety-
mology of the word, is simply rational discourse about God. But there are
many different ways of engaging in rational discourse about God. Consequently, the intellectual discipline and academic field of theology is nowadays often
thought of as divided into various specialties, which are distinguished on the
basis of their varying aims, emphases and methods. There exist, for example,
such specialized areas as *biblical theology*, whose focus is on the identification
of the precise ideas to be found in the various documents of the Bible, *historical
theology*, whose concern is to trace the development of religious thought and
doctrine through the centuries, and *systematic theology*, whose task is to
integrate into a coherent whole a wide array of fundamental beliefs concerning
God and the proper human relation to him.[1]

Our main area of inquiry in this book is in many ways appropriately thought
of as another specialized branch of theology, although, given its approach, it
is just as truly a proper part of philosophy. The aim of *philosophical theology* is
to employ the best of philosophical methods and techniques for the purpose

of gaining as much clarity as possible concerning the content of the major concepts, presuppositions, and tenets of theological commitment, as well as the many connections that exist among them. In doing philosophical theology, we ask such questions as these: Can a logically coherent conception of God be articulated? What is the ultimate source for our idea of God? What can be said about the range of God's power? How can we understand the nature of his knowledge? What is divine creation? How is God related to time? These are the sorts of questions typically investigated in philosophical theology.[2]

The enterprise of philosophically reflecting on basic questions concerning God could, in principle, be pursued in any theistic religious tradition, any tradition affirming the existence of a divine being. On many issues which arise concerning God, there are significant areas of agreement among the best philosophers within the differing faith communities of Judaism, Christianity and Islam. There are also striking points of contact with certain Hindu thinkers. In this book, however, our focus will be on the philosophically rich tradition of Christian theism which is grounded in the biblical revelation. Our primary task will be to investigate whether a conception of God can be articulated which is both philosophically plausible and biblically faithful.

The Possibility of Theology
Many perceptive thinkers throughout the centuries have worried about the very possibility of engaging in truly rational and accurate discourse about so ultimate a subject as God. Some have feared the topic to be too exalted for any reliable human cognition whatsoever. In the fourth century B.C., Plato had a character in one of his most influential dialogues say that "the father and maker of all this universe is past finding out."[3] Others have despaired over our ability even to arrive at an adequate definition of the word 'God.' In the fourth century A.D., the important Christian theologian Gregory Nazianzus once wrote: "It is difficult to conceive God, but to define him in words is an impossibility."[4] In our own day, one writer has stated that "God is ultimately profound Mystery and utterly escapes our every effort to grasp or comprehend him."[5]

If these worries and negative pronouncements are well founded, the prospects for philosophical theology are dim indeed. If God is so far beyond us as to elude all our attempts at conceptualization and definition, if he is truly "past finding out," then all attempts at engaging in rational discourse about God will be destined to fail. In order to evaluate, in at least a preliminary way, the prospects for theology in general, and for philosophical theology in particular, we must seek to determine what the source is for all this general *theological pessimism*. Fortunately, I think the basic sources of worry are fairly easy to locate and assess.

Traditional theists typically characterize God as, among other things, an all-powerful, all-knowing, perfectly good, eternal and transcendent being who has created our entire universe and preserves its existence moment to moment. As creator of the world, God is by nature not himself a thing in the world which we can perceive with our bodily senses. And as the bearer of all these extraordinary, exalted properties, God would have to be very different from all those things in his created world with which we are familiar. Each of these features of God, as traditionally thought of—his distinctness from any perceptible thing in the world and dissimilarity to anything in the world—has given rise to an argument or reason for thinking that God must ultimately be recognized to be beyond the conceptual grasp of us his creatures.

Let's consider first the claim that as creator of the world, God himself is not a thing of the world. On most traditional views, God is not a thing located in space and time. God does not have shape, size, color or hardness. He does not have mass or momentum, and is not by nature in any way directly perceptible to the bodily senses through which we acquire knowledge. But those senses are also the means by which we acquire our most basic concepts. Because of this, some people have concluded that no human concepts can possibly apply to God. They seem to reason roughly as follows, very simply:

(1) Human concepts have been developed to apply to things of the world.
(2) God is not a thing of the world.

So

(3) Human concepts cannot apply to God.[6]

Is this a good argument? In order to evaluate it, consider a parallel argument:

(1′) Teflon was developed to apply to problems in the space program.

(2') The problem of how to fry a good omelet is not a problem in the space program.

So

(3') Teflon cannot apply to the problem of how to fry a good omelet.

This second argument is clearly a bad one, since it leads from two true premises to an obviously false conclusion. The form of inference here, the pattern of reasoning employed, is thus an unreliable one. But it is of exactly the same form as our original argument. That argument is therefore a bad one as well. Both arguments can move from their two premises to their respective conclusions only by employing something like the following general suppressed premise:

(SP) For every x and every y, if x was not developed to apply to y, then x cannot apply to y,

which is an obvious falsehood. So we do not have here any good reason for believing that human concepts cannot apply to God and that theology is thus an impossible project.

At this juncture, a general point should be made concerning human concepts, and human language in general. An argument such as the one we have just examined can arise out of the belief that the sole possible function of at least the descriptive forms of human language is to encode previous experience. If human language was developed to encode our experience of the physical world, and God is not an item in the physical world, it can be inferred from this perspective that human language cannot apply to God, whatever the weaknesses of the general proposition (SP) just noted.

But it cannot be the case that language just encodes previous experience. If it did only that, we would never be able to describe a new experience without inventing a new word. Any kind or degree of novelty in experience would require new linguistic coinage. And if all that language of a descriptive sort served to do was to encode previous experience, we could never communicate with another person, because, presumably, two different people never have a strictly identical history of experiences. Human language is rather an inherently flexible device, or an array of such devices.

Some experiences may be so radically new and different as to be ineffable, or inexpressible in existent language. We have to acknowledge this possibility. And some experience of the divine has been said by the great mystics to be like this—utterly ineffable. It would be unreasonable to think that all creaturely experiences of God would easily lend themselves to clear conceptualization in existing language. But it is one thing to say that some experience of God is, or even is bound to be, ineffable, and quite another to say that God is always and altogether beyond human description.

Some theological skeptics say that no human concepts can apply to God because

(A) God is unlike anything in the world

in virtue of his extremely different ontological status, or stature in the realm of existence.[7] Two beings differ in ontological status just in case they are fundamentally different kinds of being, in the sense that what it is for one of them to exist (the conditions and nature of its existence) is quite unlike what it is for the other to exist. Beethoven's Fifth Symphony, Beethoven's birthday and Beethoven's favorite pair of boots differ rather dramatically in ontological status. But each of these things has whatever ontological status it has within the realm of human experience, and within the bounds of the history of life within our physical universe. The theological skeptic believes we run into trouble when we attempt to wander too far from these borders and seek to speak, for example, of an uncreated creator of all else, utterly transcendent to this universe. According to the skeptic, such a being would be as different from everything in our world as it is possible to be. But a single concept can apply to two different things only if those things are alike. Since all human concepts either apply to things in the world or are built up out of component concepts which apply to things in the world, if God is radically enough unlike anything in the world, and if this is because of what God and things of the world are by nature, then we indeed must conclude that human concepts cannot in fact apply to God.

We should first acknowledge here that there is an important sense in which (A) is true. God is unlike anything in the world—nothing is his match or equal.

But the sense in which (A) is true must be clarified precisely, for (A) is ambiguous between

(A1) God is not completely like anything in the world
and
(A2) God is completely unlike everything in the world.

But (A1) and (A2) express very different propositions. Most traditional theists, and Christian theists in particular, hold that (A1) is true, but that (A2) is false. The ambiguity of (A) turns on the difference between (A1) and (A2). And the difference between (A1) and (A2) is like that between

(B1) God does not share *all* properties with anything else
and
(B2) God does not share *any* properties with anything else.

It is sometimes easy to miss this difference, because it is sometimes easy to confuse 'all' and 'any.' Consider for example the two sentences

'Eat *all* the cookies you want'
'Eat *any* cookies you want'

which can both be used colloquially to say basically the same thing. But in many circumstances the difference between otherwise similar, contextualized uses of 'all' and 'any' can be quite important. Compare, for instance, the two sentences

'It is safe to take *any* of these medicines before bedtime'
'It is safe to take *all* of these medicines before bedtime.'

The difference between them could be fatal. In our case, (A1) and (B1) are compatible with the rosiest prospects for theology. Only (A2) and (B2) are such that their truth would prevent any rational human discourse about God. But (A2) could be true only if (B2) were true. And (B2) is impossible. It can't possibly be true. Let's see why.

If God and worldly things could share *no* properties in common, due to their difference in ontological status, due to the extreme difference in the kinds of beings they are, then, contrary to this supposition, they would then have to share at least one property in common:

(P) The property of having a set of properties not shared by some being with a very different ontological status.

But, that is to say, it would be possible for God and worldly things to share *no* properties in common, due to their difference in ontological status, only if they did share at least (P) in common. In other words, the claim is true only if it is false, from which we can conclude that it is impossible for it to be true. It is impossible for God and things of the world to share literally *no* properties in common. So (B2), a claim about God's radical difference which would block the possibility of doing theology if it were true, cannot possibly be true.

And, likewise, consider the main, extreme conceptual claim definitive of theological pessimism:

(TP) No human concepts can apply to God.

If (TP) were true, if *no* human concepts could apply to God, then at least *one* human concept would *have* to apply to him, namely,

(C) The concept of being such as to escape characterization by human concepts,

from which it follows that (TP) itself cannot possibly be true. Some human concepts must apply to God.

But the theological pessimist is not so easily defeated. For he can respond that if the only concepts which apply to God are like (C), then again the prospects for any interesting or extended theological knowledge are blocked from the outset. Perhaps it was logically rash for the pessimist to think that literally *no* human concepts can apply to God, but if God is so very different from anything in the world, which all traditional theists affirm, then why should we think that any *substantive* human concepts like power, goodness and knowledge apply to God? It may be that logic itself forces us to recognize the applicability of some basic human concepts to God—he is identical with himself, he is at least as great as himself, he is such that $2 + 2 = 4$, he is nonidentical with anything distinct from himself—but these concepts are hardly enough for the needs of the religious life. From them alone we could get nothing remotely resembling a creed. Concepts such as these will apply equally to any being whatsoever, and thus can indicate nothing distinctive about God. The theological pessimist who is logically astute can be thought of as a person who believes that no more than this is possible.

But what grounds could a theological pessimist have for holding such a view? To claim that God escapes characterization by most substantive, informative human concepts is to make a fairly weighty claim which itself seems to imply or presuppose some pretty important knowledge about God. We have seen that the most extreme theological pessimism falls to a *logical* difficulty. And I think it is even easier to see that this less extreme form of theological pessimism falls to an *epistemological* difficulty (one having to do with grounds or reasons for belief). For if what we might call *moderate theological pessimism* were true, how could any of us know it to be true? It would seem that a certain amount of knowledge of God, and thus a certain amount of applicability to God of substantive, informative, nontrivial human concepts, would be required in order for us to have any good grounds for such a sweeping view of deity as that presented by a moderate theological pessimism. Thus, it seems that even a moderate theological pessimism is epistemologically self-defeating. It denies the conditions under which alone we could have any reason to think its content, and thus its denials, to be true. It has the odd characteristic of being such that if it were true, we could have no good grounds for thinking it true.

Some theologians, impressed by the extreme difference of the divine, have taken a different tack here. They have not made the extreme and logically incoherent claim that no human concepts can apply to God. Nor have they made the more moderate claim just examined that no substantive, informative human concepts can hold true of deity. Rather they have endorsed *negative theology*, the *via negativa* ("the negative way") concerning the things of God. This approach to theology does not deny that human concepts of any sort can be applied to God, it just consists in the claim that human concepts can be applied to God only negatively. That is to say, only negations or denials can be made about God literally and truly. We cannot, on this view, say what God *is*, only what he is *not*. We can say that he is not a body, that he is not limited by time, that he is not restricted in power, or knowledge, or presence, or goodness. According to the *via negativa*, the main point of all the attributes traditionally associated with God—omnipotence, omniscience, omnipresence, timelessness, etc.—is that they deny limitations of God. It is in what they deny or negate, not in what they affirm, that traditional claims about God convey knowledge. Such is the central contention of the *via negativa*.

This is a position which reached its pinnacle of expression in the work of the great twelfth-century Jewish philosopher Moses Maimonides. It has also been associated to some extent with the writings of the well-known Christian mystic Meister Eckhart, and the great Islamic philosopher Avicenna. Its truth would severely restrict the prospects for philosophical theology, but it too is a view which is quite hard to defend. How can we ever be justified in saying what something is *not* unless we have some sense of what it *is*? This one question reveals the weakness endemic to any severely, or exclusively, negative theology. Rational denial seems clearly to presuppose rational affirmation. Knowledge of what something is not seems to be based upon knowledge of what, to some extent, it is. So, as a suggestion which threatens to undermine the possibility of substantive and positively informative theological discourse, the strict *via negativa* seems unconvincing.

Despite the worries they have caused many thinkers of the past, none of these attempts to debar us from the possibility of engaging in positive, rational discourse about God can be judged a success. On close examination, they seem to present no insurmountable obstacles to our approaching an investigation of the divine with some degree of confidence. Yet, as all the great theologians have realized to some extent, any confidence we do have here must be tempered by an appropriate degree of intellectual humility, as we approach what is indeed an exalted and ultimate subject.

Our Grounds for Proceeding

It is one thing to turn back various challenges to the possibility of doing theology in a positive mode. It is another matter altogether to locate some ground for confidence in our abilities here. Despite our ability to resist various forms of theological skepticism and negativity, how can we think we can even begin to approach knowledge concerning the ultimate source of all? On what basis can we come to believe that enough human concepts and language can apply to God to make possible a substantive grasp of things divine? In dealing with ultimate religious matters, we are dealing with the extraordinary, with matters much higher and deeper than those we ordinarily contemplate. This much must be admitted by anyone. So in attempting to know God, in attempting to discourse rationally about God, we most likely will have to stretch our cognitive abilities to their maximum extent. We should not expect it to be very easy. Nor should we be surprised that in order to stretch our cognitive grasp, we may occasionally have to stretch our concepts and our ordinary language far beyond the circumstances of their usual employment.

A number of the finest practitioners of philosophical theology have appreciated this point. St. Thomas Aquinas, for example, focussed on the role of analogy in our attempts to describe the divine. Other philosophers have talked of distinctively religious symbolism, and the role of metaphor in theological language. All these theorists have appreciated the potential difficulty of the conceptual task facing theology.[8] For success, we shall have to extend our conceptual structures far beyond the ordinary sphere of their employment.

But is human language and thought flexible enough for this sort of stretching? I think we have some reason to believe the answer is yes. For consider the fact that in many other realms of human cognitive endeavor, ordinary language successfully bridges the common and the extraordinary, the familiar and the extremely unfamiliar. Well-known examples of this are to be found in such diverse areas as contemporary physics and gourmet wine tasting. We do not have language ready-made for all the discoveries of physicists or all the discriminations of the palate. But we learn to use what we have in novel ways, and do so successfully. So there is some general ground for optimism concerning the flexibility and potential reach of human concepts. But why think that we can stretch our cognitive and linguistic grasp so far as to be able to comprehend something so utterly different as God?

In the biblical world-view, there is no metaphysical gap as great as that between the divine creator of all and any of his creations. But within this world view there is also a deeply imbedded belief that between God and at least one sort of creature, there is an important point of contact. For it is a central biblical belief that human beings have been created "in the image of God."[9] Of course, the precise meaning of this has been a matter of dispute. But any reasonable interpretation will hold that between whatever is characteristic of the best of human existence, and whatever is distinctive of God, there is a deeply-lying consonance. Many commentators hold that the moral, spiritual and intellectual capacities of humans, together with their creative employment, are what reflect or image the divine.

If God is infinite Mind and has brought into existence minded creatures in his image, then it might be expected that those creatures' minds could grasp something of his existence and nature. But this tentative expectation is boosted to a degree of confident anticipation by another biblical doctrine—the doctrine that we have been created by a perfectly good and loving God for the purpose of having communion with him. It is impossible to have communion with a being whose existence and nature are totally inscrutable, or incomprehensible. So the biblical understanding of the creation of human beings generates a confidence in our ability to use our linguistic and conceptual capacities to come to know our creator.

But don't the doctrines of the *imago dei* (the image of God), and the purpose of human creation already *presuppose* that we can have substantive knowledge of God? They seem clearly to do this, and if so, then they cannot be appealed to in a noncircular argument for this *theological optimism* as a conclusion.

First, it must be pointed out that the possibility of any kind of basic knowledge cannot be demonstrated by means of noncircular, nonquestion-begging arguments, by arguments that do not in any way already presume to some extent that to which they intend to lend some support. The unavailability of any such noncircular argument for the possibility of theological knowledge would thus not render theology a suspect cognitive enterprise. And, indeed, it is true that the appeal to biblical doctrines such as those I have mentioned cannot constitute a noncircular argument. If we didn't think we could have substantive knowledge of God, and if we didn't take ourselves to have any reason for believing that we do have such knowledge, we would have no reason for thinking these doctrines to be true. These doctrines thus presuppose some degree of theological optimism. But they also play an interesting role in laying out possible grounds for defending that presupposition and for understanding how in fact it can be true. Theological optimism is as much a presupposition of theological activity as some degree of scientific optimism is of scientific activity. In much the same way that many of the early modern scientists, the members of the British Royal Society in the eighteenth century, for example, approached nature with confidence because of their belief that nature had been brought into existence by a rational creator who would not have placed us in an environment we could not understand, so also many philosophers and theologians approach a study of divinity with similar confidence. If a rational God has created us as rational beings lovingly intended for fellowship with him, then we should confidently expect to be able to come to know something of his existence and nature. We should expect the cognitive apparatus with which we have been endowed to be up to the task, however intellectually daunting it might initially seem.

But the proof is in the testing. It is one thing to resist the theological pessimist, and even to sketch out possible grounds for theological optimism, it is another to come to see that such optimism is indeed well founded. *Can* substantive human concepts apply to God? Can we come to have knowledge of God's nature? The only way to answer these questions for ourselves is to try and see. Will we find all our attempts to speak of God thwarted by obscurity, mystery, paradox and contradiction? Or, on the contrary, will we find our efforts enjoying apparent success, corroborating our initial confidence, our optimism about the theological project? Only an exercise such as that attempted by this book will tell. Among contemporary philosophers there is some measure of disagreement, although, as I shall attempt to indicate throughout, I think we have increasing grounds for a measured optimism concerning the traditional enterprise of theology. We should never expect to arrive at complete or comprehensive knowledge concerning God. But ultimate incompleteness of information is compatible here, as it often is elsewhere, with much correctness of belief.

2

The Concept
of God

*I*n the fifth century B.C., the Greek poet Pindar posed the question "What is God?" and presented the answer "Everything." Whatever its intellectual merits, given the time and place of its utterance, this answer considered by Pindar was clearly not a very discriminating response. Nor was it a claim that would be accepted by many traditional religious believers.

The view which seems to have been expressed so succinctly by Pindar, the belief that God is everything or, as it is more typically stated, the belief that everything is God, is usually called *pantheism*. Most religious people, at least most people within the more advanced religious traditions of the world, have used the word 'God' and its correlates in other languages not to refer in this way to everything in general, but rather to refer only to something in particular, something quite ultimate, a being on whom we and our world depend. This is the religious view known as *theism*, the belief in a God distinct from all other things. Any belief that there are two or more such beings independent of one another, and each properly considered divine, is a brand of *polytheism*. The belief that there is only one ultimate divine being, the conviction proclaimed in one way or another by Judaism, Christianity and Islam, is called *monotheism*.

Throughout human history, there have been many different conceptions of the divine. And this fact in itself poses us a problem. The problem is not just how we can arrive at our own idea of God. The problem is how we can arrive at the best idea of God, a conception worthy of our greatest energies, intellectual and otherwise.

The Problem of Method

When we reflect on ultimate religious issues, what precise concept of deity will we be employing? And how can this be decided? With this latter question, we confront the premier problem of method in philosophical theology. Is there some single method for arriving at an idea of God? And if so, then why are there so many differences among people as to how we should describe the divine? Are there rather many different rival methods for arriving at a basic conception of deity? And if there are, which method is to be preferred? How is this issue to be decided? Is there a way of rationally choosing a best method for thinking about God? Before we can hope to make any real progress in our attempt to think about God, we must confront this barrage of questions and seek to determine whether they can be answered with any significant degree of confidence.

In every science, the issue of method is of great importance. For without a reliable method of discovery or testing, we can never be confident of our ability to attain reliable beliefs, and thus knowledge, in any such area, where we are moving beyond the bounds of immediate experience. Individual sciences have begun to flourish only as their practitioners have come to agree on the appropriateness and basic trustworthiness of particular methods for dealing with their most fundamental problems. And in so far as theology, in its own unique way, purports to be, in effect, a science of God and things divine, it too must face and grapple with the issue of method if it is to flourish.

Intelligent and rational disagreement of any kind presupposes some level of agreement or shared understanding. A disagreement, for instance, over who is currently the best tennis player in the world will typically presuppose at least some basic agreement over what the game of tennis is, and thus over what sort of people are to count as tennis players. Theists and atheists disagree over whether there is a God. Christians and non-Christians often disagree over whether the story of Jesus is a true story of God living among us as a human being. In order for these disagreements to be intelligent and rational, the theist and the atheist must both have in mind some single idea of God, and so must the Christian and his non-Christian interlocutor. Otherwise, one party would not be denying what the other party is affirming. If they were not operating, at least at some level, with the same idea of God, however rough-edged or vague, their specific disagreements could not even be formulated. We can think of the theist as believing that some particular idea of God is successfully reality-depicting. Along the same lines, we can think of the atheist who is in disagreement with him as believing that *the same idea of God* fails to be truly reality-depicting.

When a Christian and a non-Christian disagree over whether the story of Jesus presents God to us in a true and particularly distinctive way, their disagreement can occur over the basic issue of whether there is a God at all. Or it can occur as a disagreement between theists—the one believing that God once took human form and came to dwell among us as Jesus, the other asserting that the God who exists did no such thing. This disagreement over Jesus could not take place as an intelligent conflict of belief without some shared understanding of the basic idea of God. And where is this idea to come from? Exactly what idea is it to be?

The theist proposes; his opponent denies. The Christian proposes; his opponent denies. As a general rule, he who proposes must explain. It is his responsibility to articulate clearly what exactly the proposal is. It is thus up to the theist, and up to the Christian, to explain what exactly is meant by the word 'God'. But of course it is presumably in the interests of all parties to such religious disputes that the best idea of God which can be formulated be the one which is introduced for discussion. And so we need to ask what procedure or method for articulating an idea of God will best provide for this sort of result.

The problem of method in philosophical theology is posed by the fact that there are, in principle, many possible methods for arriving at, or articulating, an idea of God. One possible way of proceeding, for example, would be to attempt to consult all the purported revelations claimed by different religious traditions throughout human history, and draw from them a composite portrait of the divine. This possible method for arriving at a determinate conception of God can be referred to as the method of *universal revelational theology*. It is a procedure which has seemed attractive to many sincere inquiring people, and even to some ecumenically minded Christians, but it is a method with at least one fundamental flaw. Many of the purported revelations of God to be found throughout human history conflict. They offer incompatible accounts of the divine. How are we supposed to separate the sheep from the goats, the wheat from the chaff? The simple, apparently open-minded method of *universal revelational theology* does not itself provide us with a criterion of selection. It is not sufficiently discriminating, however ecumenically attractive it initially might appear to some people.

What is needed is a touchstone for theological acceptability, a standard, a measuring stick, a reliable guide for constructing our idea of God, a criterion which will help us avoid inconsistency. And of course, Christians have traditionally taken the Bible to provide exactly this.[1] Some Christian theologians have gone on to insist that the Bible provides us with our only fully reliable source of knowledge about God. In line with this, they sometimes go on to the extreme of recommending a distinct method for articulating a basic conception of deity which we can call, quite simply, *purely biblical theology*.[2] The guiding principle of this method is that we should go to the Bible, and only to the Bible, for our idea of God.

One problem for purely biblical theology is that, despite some theologians' claims to follow its strictures, it is not clear that anyone can manage to do so if they are seeking a philosophically adequate conception of the divine. The rule definitive of this method, as I understand it here, is that we should think or say about God only what is explicitly said about him in the Bible, or in addition what is strictly, logically implied by what the Bible manifestly contains. The reason why no philosopher or theologian seeking a philosophically adequate conception of God can manage finally to adhere to this rule is that, in our capacity of asking philosophical questions about the nature of God, we inevitably ask questions the biblical documents were not designed to answer.

The Bible is not a textbook of philosophical theology. Its texts on God are thus neither as complete nor as specific as the philosophical theologian needs in order to be able to answer fully his conceptual, or philosophical, questions.

Are these philosophical questions then illegitimate from a biblical standpoint? I see no reason to think so at all. From the fact that the biblical documents, written as they were to deal with burning practical questions of the greatest personal significance, do not address all the possible philosophical questions which can also, in their own way, be of the greatest intellectual significance, it does not follow at all that these more theoretical questions are illegitimate, or that they are unimportant. They can be quite important for the constructing of any comprehensive Christian world-view, and answers to them can help us to understand more deeply the biblical answers to more immediately practical questions. It can even be argued that it is incumbent upon any intelligent person who finds himself asking philosophical questions about matters of religious belief to do whatever it is in his power to do in order to find answers to them. Otherwise, such a person may be blocked from responding to God as a believer in the full integrity of his personality. It is never incumbent upon a Christian to eschew the quest for understanding, even when it leads him beyond the letter of the commitments of the Bible.

The challenge for the Christian philosopher or theologian should not be that of confining what he says about God to what the Bible has already said, but rather it should be that of constructing a philosophical theology which is thoroughly consonant with the biblical portrayal of God. What should be sought are not just philosophical ideas which happen to be logically consistent, or minimally compatible, with the biblical materials, but rather ideas which are deeply attuned to the biblical revelation, and thus consonant with the whole tenor of the Bible.

But if we are to build on the ideas of the Bible, we need a further method. We need a biblically based theology which is not as restrictive as the method of purely biblical theology. We need a method for drawing from, elaborating upon, and augmenting the content of the biblical materials in a way that will allow us to address any important philosophical issues concerning the nature of God which were not given fully developed answers by the biblical authors.

Some philosophers have suggested that the central idea of the Bible is its presentation of God as our creator, and as the creator of our world. It has also been said that the most central characterization of God in the Bible is its portrayal of him as the creator of all. In connection with these claims, we need to consider a method for thinking about deity which we can call *creation theology*. This method for articulating a conception of God centers around the claim that God is to be understood as the ultimate creator of every reality which exists distinct from himself. The precise method to be employed in connection with this claim is then explanatory in nature.

In this method for articulating a concept of God, it is said that, in order to explain the existence and nature of our universe, we must postulate the existence of a cause whose nature and activity would be sufficient for the production of such an astounding effect as the entire physical cosmos, with all its denizens, must be considered to be. Thus, according to the method of creation theology, the concept of God is properly taken to be the concept of a being who can serve the theoretical role of such an explanation.

As a way of thinking about God, creation theology has much to recommend it. First, as we have suggested, it has strong revelational backing. And second, it has seemed to many people to be an eminently rational method of thought. Indeed, it seems to consist in a procedure of postulational reasoning which, as used in the natural sciences, has proved its value time and again as a method of intellectual discovery: to explain the existence, occurrence or behavior of *A* we postulate the existence, occurrence or behavior of *B;* we postulate only what is strictly required for explaining *A,* and by so doing we quite often arrive at what is later confirmed as the truth. This method of thinking thus often appeals to people who consider themselves to be of a tough-minded, hard-nosed, scientific mindset. Even philosophers dubious of any claims to revelation, and thus disinclined to grant any special philosophical significance to the Bible as a source of ideas can find themselves strongly attracted to this basic method for articulating a concept of divinity. It seems to be a procedure which rationally can stand on its own.

But as a sole, independent method for articulating a conception of God, creation theology looks frustratingly incomplete. The idea of God arising exclusively out of this sort of explanatory reasoning inevitably has a rather minimal content which is both religiously and philosophically unsatisfying.

Any being whose creative activity could explain adequately the existence of our universe would presumably have to be extraordinarily powerful and knowledgeable. But exactly how much power and knowledge should we think of him as enjoying? Creation theology will direct us to conceive of God as having enough power to create this cosmos. It will license us to ascribe to God at least this much power. But the problem is that a great many theists have wanted to ascribe to God the power to have created other sorts of universes instead, universes with more objects or with different kinds of objects. The belief is that he did not exhaust his power in his creation of this universe. Can creation theology authorize such a belief? It is hard to see how. And even if it could, it seems beyond the range of its method to specify exactly how much superabundant power God has.

And what of God's character? Is there enough evidence in the existence and nature of the universe to warrant fully the postulation of the idea of God as a morally perfect creator? In view of all the evil in the world—the pain, suffering and injustice—it would seem not. At least, it would be extremely difficult if possible at all to arrive at such an idea from nothing more than an explanatory extrapolation from our world. And yet this is something most theists would endorse as a central component in their idea of God.

There are two simple ways to augment creation theology in order to attempt to alleviate these inadequacies. First, for those who are suspicious of claims to revelation and who thus want to employ this sort of method on its own, it is possible to see creation theology as only the initial impetus to, and a mere partial application of, a broader *comprehensive explanatory theology*, a method which would take as its data to be explained not only the existence and basic nature of our universe, but also all those occurrences in human history deemed to be of religious significance: apparent miracles, signs of providential intent, and various sorts of religious experience. An explanatory method which casts its net more broadly in this way can be expected to arrive at a correspondingly more finely specified final explanation or explanatory postulation.

Although this broadening of method would probably result in some improvement, it is a bit difficult to see how it would help in resolving the specific questions which have been raised. Some idea of divine character in relation to humans could be hypothesized, but the result would probably still fall far short of the extreme claims theists, and in particular Christian theists, have thought it important to make for God. And there is no evident way at all that this broadening could deal with the problem of specifying the full degree of power enjoyed by God. So a good deal of incompleteness would still remain.

We should not forget, however, that we introduced the method of creation theology as a biblically based idea. As the psalmist wrote, "The heavens declare the glory of God, and the firmament proclaims his handiwork" (Ps 19:1). If it, or even its broader relative, is thought of as a method for augmenting the descriptions of God already to be found in the Bible, it matters somewhat less what this method, operating under its own steam, can produce. Its results are automatically viewed as augmented by what the Bible already contains, and when it comes to questions about the character of God, that augmentation is considerable. For the God of the Bible is "righteous and upright" (Deut 32:4), "gracious and compassionate, slow to anger, abounding in lovingkindness" (Joel 2:13); "all his works are truth, and his ways justice" (Dan 4:37); "great is the LORD, and greatly to be praised" (Ps 48:1).

But questions still remain unanswered. Even a biblically based creation theology, or a broader, biblically based comprehensive explanatory theology, seem to leave certain central and relevant philosophical questions about the nature of God unanswered. How do we specify the precise scope of God's power and knowledge, the full strength of his character, the mode of his being or the nature of his reality? The Bible clearly points us in a certain direction, toward an exalted, ultimate conception of God. It just does not address all our relevant philosophical questions. Both creation theology and comprehensive explanatory theology offer us help in that regard. But they too, for all their value, seem to stop short of providing sufficient guidance for dealing with all our legitimate questions about the grandeur of deity. So the issue naturally arises: Is there a method which is both revelational and rational, compatible with both the insights of the Bible and sound explanatory methods, which will offer, in principle, a complete philosophical perspective on God, and thus will result in the best conception of God we can attain? An idea stated quite succinctly by Saint Anselm, archbishop of Canterbury (A.D. 1033-1109), can be taken to have provided us with at least the elements of just that sort of method, if properly understood and developed.

Perfect Being Theology

According to Anselm, God is to be thought of most fundamentally as "that than which no greater can be conceived."[3] Most contemporary philosophers have taken Anselm's basic idea here to be best interpreted to mean that God is to be thought of as *the greatest possible being,* an individual exhibiting *maximal perfection.* This core conception of deity is both very general and at the same time highly focused. It does not explicitly give us many specifics concerning God, hence its generality. But it provides a single focus for all our reflections about divinity, one point of light to guide all our thinking about the nature of God. The idea of God as the greatest possible being is not itself a full-blown conception of deity; rather, it is more like the main element in a recipe for cooking up our idea of God in detail. This core idea, along with an accompanying method for its development, will be what constitutes Anselm's most distinctive contribution to religious thinking, the philosophical procedure known as *perfect being theology.*

The ideas to be found in perfect being theology are not altogether original with Anselm. The conception of God as unsurpassably great is clearly itself a central biblical idea. But what Anselm provided was a precise philosophical statement of that idea and an examination of some of its implications. It was thus Anselm who pioneered the clarification and use of this biblically based and philosophically attuned method of thinking about God.

We can characterize the core of perfect being theology as the thesis that:

(G) God is a being with the greatest possible array of compossible great-making properties.

Clearly, the terms in this thesis require some elucidation. A *great-making property* is any property, or attribute, or characteristic, or quality which it is intrinsically good to have, any property which endows its bearer with some measure of value, or greatness, or metaphysical stature, regardless of external circumstances. The key idea here is of course that of *intrinsic goodness.* By contrast, *extrinsic goodness* has to do with value determined by external relations or outward circumstances. For example, if there is a sniper on the roof of my office building prepared to shoot anyone who leaves during the next hour, then the property of staying inside this building for more than an hour is a good property or attribute for me to have. But its value clearly depends entirely on external circumstances.

Very often, when we say of something that it is good, what we mean is that it is extrinsically good. Some nutritionists and physicians tell us nowadays that the habit of eating oatmeal for breakfast almost every morning is a good thing. But this surely has nothing to do with the intrinsic experience or event of eating oatmeal. Eating oatmeal regularly is *good* only because it is *good for* maintaining low blood cholesterol. And maintaining low blood cholesterol is in turn a good thing because it is good for avoiding heart trouble and maintaining general good health. It will help us to get a precise philosophical grasp of extrinsic goodness and its relation to intrinsic goodness if we symbolize the conditions under which claims to goodness hold true.

When it is said of some object, or property, A, that A is extrinsically good, what is really meant is that having A or standing in some particular relation to A is good for standing in some distinct relation R to some object or state of affairs B, something extrinsic or external to A. To say that A is *good for* this is to say that standing in the right relation to A is conducive to, or productive of, this further relation. But then we will in this way think of A as good or a good only if we also think of standing in R to B as itself a good thing. And if we here again have in mind extrinsic goodness, then standing in R to B must in turn be good for standing in some further relation $R1$ to some object C. That's just what extrinsic goodness requires, as we have seen. Let 'P' name the property of standing in relation R to object B, and '$P1$' name the property of standing in $R1$ to C. In the realm of extrinsic goodness, P will be thought of as good in so far as, and only in so far as, it leads to $P1$. But this will make no sense unless $P1$ is itself judged a good thing. And if this judgment is again one of extrinsic goodness, then $P1$ must be good in virtue of leading to some further relation $R2$ to some object C, the property of standing in which we can denote as '$P2$.'

What we are now in position to see is something very interesting. Some modern philosophers with world views very different from Anselm's have thought that all goodness is extrinsic, and thus that there is nothing which is intrinsically good. If this were true, then perfect being theology could not even get off the ground, for there would be no great-making properties to attribute to God. But could all goodness be extrinsic goodness? It seems highly problematic to think so, for supposing this to be true lands us in a perplexing dilemma. If all goodness is extrinsic goodness, then P cannot be good unless it leads to $P1$, which cannot be good unless it in turn leads to some value-endowing $P2$, which itself cannot be good or a source of value unless it leads to some value-endowing $P3$, and so forth. At some point, either we arrive at a value-endowing Pn which is identical with some earlier Pn-m, in which case we are faced with a perplexing circularity of explanation, or else there never arises such an identity, in which case we are faced with what philosophers call an "infinite regress" of explanations. But to be posed with the prospect that all ascriptions of goodness are either circular or infinitely complex is to be posed with an unsatisfying dilemma.

The other possibility, the alternative envisioned by Anselm and many theists, is that some things are intrinsically good, good in themselves, and thus are proper ultimate stopping points in explanations of goodness. That is to say, the recognition of something as an intrinsic good can be an appropriate terminus, or endpoint, to any explanation of value. Thus, a conception of value which countenances intrinsic as well as extrinsic values would seem to be more intellectually or rationally satisfying than one endorsing only extrinsic value. And it is just such a broader conception of value which Anselm's understanding of God requires.

So a great-making property is to be thought of as a property it is intrinsically good to have. And the core thesis of perfect being theology, proposition (G), ascribes to God the greatest possible array of *compossible* great-making properties. An array or collection of properties is compossible just in case it is possible that they all be had by the same individual at the same time, or all together. A simple example of a pair of noncompossible properties would be the property of being married and the property of being a bachelor. Knowledge and benevolence, on the other hand, are compossible properties. If God is thought of as having the greatest possible array of compossible great-making properties, we are thinking of God's nature as consisting in a cluster of properties intrinsically good to have, properties which can all be exemplified together, and which are such that their additive value, as a group, is unsurpassable by any other possible array of great-making properties. And if God is being thought of singularly as *the* greatest possible being, he is thought to be the sole possessor of such an array of properties. He is being thought of as being so great that no other, independent being could possibly rival him in greatness. With this, we arrive at the supreme conception of perfection, and moreover at the greatest possible idea that a human being could ever entertain. For what idea could possibly be greater than the idea of a unique, greatest possible being, necessarily without peer?

But we are still at a level of high abstraction and generality here. We are in need of more specifics. We have at this point only the core of a detailed conception of deity. To begin to fill out this conception of the divine, to employ the full method of perfect being theology, we need to begin to consult our value intuitions. What properties can we intuitively recognize as great-making properties, and what clusters of properties can be seen likewise to correspond to a high value, or an exalted metaphysical stature? It is part of the method of perfect being theology for us to consult our intuitions on these matters. It is one of the assumptions of this method that there will be at least widespread agreement among people who are rightly positioned and well disposed concerning at least many such intuitions.

Now, it should be pointed out that by the word 'intuition' we do not necessarily mean to denote here some mysterious faculty for information gathering. Nor do we refer to anything which is an infallible guide to truth. Intuition is much more commonplace than that. Someone intuitively judges a proposition or claim to be true just in case, on merely considering the proposition, or the content of the claim, it appears true to him, and that appearance does not derive entirely from either perceptual belief-forming mechanisms (such as sight, hearing or smell) or from mere definitional conventions (from our human decisions) to use a word to have a certain meaning, as could be the case in the proposition: *The sentence "A triangle is a closed plane figure with three straight sides" expresses a truth.* Simply put, an intuitively formed belief seems to be a sort of naturally formed belief, a belief whose acceptance does not derive entirely from linguistic definition, evidence, testimony, memory, inference or sense experience. Our intuitions are among our most basic judgments about the world around us. We intuitively judge that 2 + 2 = 4, that nothing could be colored without being extended, that the basic properties of matter are the same in different regions of the universe, that there are some fundamental principles of logical reasoning which are reliable, and that it is wrong to torture innocent people for no reason. And these are just a few examples. We could not even begin to use logic, mathematics or scientific method without an intuitive judgment that their most basic assumptions, propositions and principles are true. Some critics ask why we should trust such intuitions, or any intuitions at all. But to ask why anyone should ever rely on intuition is like asking why anyone should ever believe what seems to him to be true. The point, however, should be made that not all intuitions are equal. It seems that there are degrees of intuitive support a proposition can have— some intuitions are just stronger than others. And some are reliable, whereas others are not. Most practitioners of perfect being theology take our intuitions about matters of value, as they do most other intuitions, to be innocent until proven guilty, or reliable until proven deceptive. The alternative is a form of skepticism with few attractions.

In order to elaborate an Anselmian idea of God, all practitioners of perfect being theology consult their value intuitions about what basic properties are great-making properties. Beginning with one of the least controversial candidates for the status of great-making property, we can represent schematically the development of a conception of a perfect being which I think would accord in one way or another with the intuitions of most of those who employ this method. In one representative example of an ascending order of discovery concerning the various aspects of his greatness in metaphysical stature, God can be conceived of in this way as:

(1) conscious (a minded being capable of and engaged in states of thought and awareness),

(2) a conscious free agent (a being capable of free action),

(3) a thoroughly benevolent, conscious agent,

(4) a thoroughly benevolent conscious agent with significant knowledge,

(5) a thoroughly benevolent conscious agent with significant knowledge and power,

(6) a thoroughly benevolent conscious agent with unlimited knowledge and power, who is the creative source of all else,

(7) a thoroughly benevolent conscious agent with unlimited knowledge and power who is the necessarily existent, ontologically independent creative source of all else.

And with this, we have arrived at what, with all its implications, is the highest conception of all, the conception of a unique, maximally perfect, or greatest possible, being. It is some such cumulative development of intuitions concerning intrinsic goodness, great-making properties, and the comparative greatness of different arrays of such properties that every practitioner of perfect being theology must undertake.

This representative list of seven stages of development in the elaboration of an Anselmian conception of God was constructed quite simply. First, it is agreed by many people that a being capable of conscious awareness is of greater intrinsic value or metaphysical stature than a thing with no such capacity, a rock for example. But then, it would be even greater not to be just a passive perceiver of things, or a conscious being confined to its own thoughts, but rather to be a conscious being capable of acting out its values and intentions into the world. And if to be an agent is good in itself, then to be an agent whose agency is thoroughly characterized by morally good or benevolent intentions is even better. Likewise, it is better for such an agent to have significant knowledge and power than to be extremely limited in these respects; and, finally, it would seem to be greater still to suffer no limits in these areas. Ultimately, a being unlimited in power and knowledge who was the source of all other beings would seem to be superior to one who, for all his excellence, was just one among other independent beings. And, at the limit of our conceptions, it would seem to be the greatest possible status to be such a being, exalted in all other respects, whose foothold in reality was so firm that it is impossible that the being not exist. Each level in our schematic ascent thus represents a development in our conception of greatness appropriate for the greatest possible being, which is God.

Questions and Refinements: The Ultimate Method

Do all practitioners of perfect being theology agree at every point concerning what God is like? Any look at the history of philosophical theology, or at the current literature on our idea of God, will show that the answer is no.[4] No method for thinking about God is a fully mechanical procedure, capable of turning out precisely the same results regardless of who employs it. There is plenty of room for disagreement among those who conceptualize God in Anselm's way, as we shall have occasion to see in later chapters.

Some philosophers think of God as timelessly eternal, an individual existing outside the bounds of time as well as space. Others conceive of God as an everlasting individual, existing throughout the entirety of time. Their disagreement can sometimes be seen to be a dispute over which of these alternate relations to time would be a more perfect form of existence. Value intuitions here and elsewhere can differ, as can intuitions over what is or is not possible. Our intuitions thus have *defeasible epistemic status.* The epistemic status of a belief or judgment is its status with respect to the goal of knowledge (in Greek, *episteme*). A belief has positive epistemic status, we can say, in case the person with the belief is justified in holding it, given the goal of attaining knowledge. But the status of a belief is defeasible in case it is possible that it be undermined or overturned. To say that our intuitions are defeasible is thus to say that, whatever positive degree of warrant or support they supply for a judgment or belief, they are in principle, and often in practice, correctable. They are not, to emphasize the point made earlier, infallible.

Our construction of an Anselmian conception of God is fueled by our value intuitions and by our modal intuitions—our intuitions concerning what is possible and impossible. But because intuitions are correctable, and because our intuitions are typically not comprehensive, that is to say, because we do not typically have intuitions clearly leading us on every issue relevant to attaining a full conception of deity which might arise, the method of perfect being theology is not in principle cut off from creative interaction with other methods for conceiving of God. And, in fact, I think it is best seen as the primary method for integrating all other plausible methods for thinking of God.

Let us first consider for a moment the fact that we do not have any reason to believe that we human beings have a comprehensive capacity for generating all the intuitions which might be needed for recognizing all the great-making properties that ought to enter into our idea of God. We thus might miss some important divine attributes if we rely upon perfect being theology and our value intuitions alone for our idea of deity. Now, some such attributes could conceivably be supplied by the method of creation theology, or the broader comprehensive explanatory theology. Consider for example the property of being powerful. Some people claim to have no value intuitions that support the judgment that this is a great-making property. They may feel that the property of being powerful is in itself, or intrinsically, value-neutral and that it can take on extrinsic value only as a function of what kind of being has the property, and how the power in question is used. If people with these judgments about power were to think about God using only the method of perfect being theology, they would have difficulty arriving at any satisfactory judgment concerning the resources and scope for divine agency. But it is a basic postulation of creation theology that God is to be thought of as having great power. The only difficulty for creation theology might be in specifying the precise extent of that power, as we have seen. But at this point, once we have granted that God has great power, the perspective of perfect being theology can kick in and specify that God's power will have no limits that imply imperfection or inferiority. His power will be viewed as being as exalted as possible. In some such way, it could be possible for perfect being theology to be supplemented by creation theology, which would then in turn be supplemented by Anselmian thinking. In this way a dynamic interaction of the two methods could be possible.

But it is also possible that our intuitions fail to settle some question about the nature of God, and the property in question is not such that it would have to be postulated as a characteristic of the divine by either creation theology or comprehensive explanatory theology. It is quite plausible to think that if there were any such divine attributes that would be important for us to know of, and yet which are such as to slip through the net of our intuitions and of our explanatory needs, God would reveal them to us. The goodness of God conceptualized by perfect being theology would seem to guarantee that. Thus, it behooves us to be open to consulting the apparent data of revelation available to us.

But even more importantly, the intuitions we do have, and the explanatory postulations we do make might not all be trustworthy. They might thus need to be corrected at the bar of special revelation. Consider as an example one particular case having to do with value intuitions. In recent years, Nicholas Wolterstorff has pointed out that many Christians, unduly influenced by ancient Stoic thought, have supposed it to be a perfection to be absolutely undisturbed by any passion or emotion whatsoever. Accordingly, they have characterized God as *impassible*, incapable of perturbation by any emotion or passion. Wolterstorff argues that this is out of step with the biblical portrayal of God as a suffering God.[5] The upshot of his argument is that some classical theological intuitions about impassibility must be corrected by the content of the biblical revelation. As the nature of Wolterstorff's case makes clear, it is possible for our value intuitions to be skewed or distorted by a dominant or powerful philosophical tradition. Any well-attested data from revelation should be allowed to overturn, or correct, contrary value intuitions such as these.

So the method of perfect being theology needs a revelational control. But it's also true that perfect being theology itself can act as an interpretive constraint on how we read the Bible. For example, from earliest times biblical commentators have assured us that when in the Old Testament the Bible speaks of "the hand of God" or "the mouth of God," we are not to suppose that God has, literally, bodily parts such as hands and a mouth. Why? Because it is more perfect not to be by nature limited to such a form of indirect agency as that of having to work by means of hands and speak by means of a mouth. The dynamic of interactions among the plausible methods for thinking about God is thus a complex matter. Each method can provide its own input data for our conception of God, and can offer constraints on the data to be gained from the other methods. For Christians, creation theology, comprehensive explanatory theology, and perfect being theology are to be endorsed in so far as they capture leading ideas or directions of thought to be found in the Bible, and provide for a philosophical extension of these ideas. Perfect being theology, capturing as it does the most majestic conception of God imaginable, rightly provides a leading method for our thinking and a touchstone for our employment and integration of the procedures of all the other plausible methods for thinking about the nature of God. In its intuitive and integrative force, I think, it is without parallel and thus properly establishes for us priorities in our conceiving of God. God is to be thought of as a being without any limitations that imply imperfection or inferiority. God is to be thought of as the greatest possible being. And he is to be conceived as the greatest possible creative source of being.

Creation theology and perfect being theology pick up on different strands of biblical thinking, strands of thought that are deeply intertwined throughout the whole history of Judeo-Christian thought. They can also be thought of as echoes of Platonism, in the case of perfect being theology, with its stress on value, and Aristotelianism, in the case of creation theology, with its emphasis on causation. Both the concern with value and the concern with causation are enduring and legitimate preoccupations within the enterprises of general philosophical reflection and theology inquiry. It is my suggestion that not only do these concerns complement one another in our thinking about God, but that, properly understood, the methods to which they give rise not only interact in a natural way, but finally coincide in their ultimate results. It can be argued that anyone who begins with creation theology and endorses a few simple and independently plausible metaphysical theses, widely endorsed by theists of all kinds throughout the centuries, will find himself with the conclusion that stands as the core of perfect being theology.[6] Simply put, if God is conceived of as, necessarily, the ultimate cause of every other being, and we endorse some principle to the effect that no effect can equal or exceed its ultimate cause in plenitude of being, or metaphysical stature, or intrinsic value, then it will follow that this creator God is the greatest possible being. That is to say, starting with creation theology can plausibly be thought to result in the endorsement of the fundamental tenet of perfect being theology, the full explication of which will require the use of its attendant method. And I think it is also quite plausible to hold that a reasonable development of perfect being theology will result in an endorsement of the core thesis of creation theology, the claim that God is the creator of anything which might exist distinct from himself. For as we have already seen while working through a representative seven-step development of the Anselmian idea of God, if we imagined any existing universe as existing wholly independent of God, as depending in no way on God for its existence and activity, it would seem that the conception of God with which we were operating was not that of a greatest possible being after all. For, surely, a being would have greater value, or greater metaphysical stature, if it was an absolute source of existence, such that nothing else could exist without deriving its reality from this being. Thus, in order for God truly to be thought of as the greatest possible being, he would also have to be thought of as what we can call an "absolute creator." Such, I think, is the link from perfect being theology to creation theology.

And once the practitioner of perfect being theology has arrived at this point, it stands to reason that he will find the method of creation theology to be important for filling out that conception of God as absolute creator. Thus, when it comes to the two distinctively philosophical methods for conceiving of God used by Christians and others through the centuries more than any other procedure, it seems reasonable to think that, regardless of which one might seem initially most attractive as a procedure, a theist will end up also endorsing the core claim and employing the procedures distinctive of the other method as well. There is something intellectually satisfying about this. For perfect being theology focuses on the intrinsic properties of God, whereas creation theology emphasizes the actual and potential relations holding between God and all else possible. They both seek, in their own ways, to explicate one important facet or another of metaphysical ultimacy, the intent they both have in common. Thus, they both can function in our attempt to articulate a philosophically adequate, as well as a biblically responsible, concept of God.

3

God's
Goodness

*T*he proclamation of God's goodness echoes throughout the pages of the Bible. In the Psalms especially we find a number of exuberant affirmations of this central divine attribute:

Good and upright is the LORD (25:8)

Oh taste and see that the LORD is good (34:8)

For the LORD is good; his mercy is everlasting (100:5).

And in the pages of the New Testament we hear Jesus say:

No one is good except God alone (Mk 10:18).

The early medieval philosopher Boethius even once went so far as to proclaim:

The substance of God consists in nothing else but in goodness.[1]

For the religious believer, trust, praise and worship all focus in on this one property, whose importance in the religious life thus cannot be overestimated. In fact, earlier in this century, the British philosopher A. C. Ewing once stated that the most important thing about religion is its claim that the being on whom everything depends is absolutely and supremely good.

It is the philosopher's job to clarify the sense, or senses, in which God is said to be good, and to explore the nature of the most central beliefs which have been held about divine goodness. We shall see that beneath the surface of this apparently simple affirmation about God lies a surprising wealth of conceptual commitments.

Perspectives on God's Goodness

In line with perfect being theology, most philosophically reflective theists have claimed that God is perfectly good. This can be understood as a twofold claim, captured in the following theses:

(1) God is wholly good,
(2) God is necessarily good.

Thesis (1) means that there is no defect or blemish in God or in his actions. He is completely, thoroughly good. On the view of divinity captured in this proposition, God never does anything which is ultimately wrong or evil. His character contains no flaw, and he is subject to no moral weakness. Thesis (2) goes further than this and holds that God is so firmly entrenched in goodness, or alternately, that goodness is so entrenched in God, that it is strictly impossible for there to be in him any sort of flaw or defect. To claim that God is necessarily good is to claim that he is utterly invulnerable to evil. It is impossible for him to do, or to be, evil. This is the most exalted view of the strength of divine goodness imaginable, and is thus thoroughly consonant with the Anselmian conception of God developed in chapter two.

Both these theses have been endorsed by a great number of theists throughout the centuries, but both have been disputed as well. Consider thesis (1), the claim that God is wholly or completely good. Some critics point to all the evil and suffering in our world and ask "How, if we think of God as the creator of this world, can we think of him as wholly good? Would not a perfectly good God create a better world?" This is the famous challenge known as the *problem of evil*. But, given the centrality of the idea of goodness in the Christian concept of God, as noted by Ewing and Boethius, the problem of evil is standardly seen as a challenge not to the claim that God should be conceived as wholly good, that complete goodness is part of the idea of God, but rather to the claim that there is in fact such a God who is responsible for the existence of our world. It is only because God is traditionally conceived of as all good, all powerful, and all knowing that the philosophical problem of evil arises in the first place. This problem does not prevent in the least our understanding (1) as a conceptual explication of the Christian idea of God.[2]

But is God portrayed in the Bible as completely good? Many critics insist that even a casual reading of the Old Testament will prove otherwise. Time and again God is represented by the biblical authors as instructing his chosen people to massacre indigenous tribes in order to conquer and control a land he has promised them. And this happens, of course, after God has plagued the Egyptians and taken the lives of all their first-born children. God demands worship and announces himself to be a jealous God (Ex 20:5; Deut 5:9). He is pictured as allowing Job to be tortured psychologically, his family killed, just to prove a point. On at least one occasion, he is reported to have engaged in a deception (1 Kings 22:23). And the great prophets themselves represent God as saying that he is responsible for evil as well as good (Is 45:7; Jer 4:6; 11:11; and elsewhere).

There are indeed numerous problematic passages in the Bible which can seem to count against the claim that the God of the Jews is wholly good. However, both Jewish and Christian theologians and biblical commentators have insisted that the clear central biblical conviction about God is that he is completely good. His revelation is true, his promises are trustworthy, he is altogether worthy of admiration and worship. The difficult passages, they argue, should therefore be interpreted in light of this clear, overwhelmingly central theme. Some of our problems here are just due to our common failure to understand the very different forms of literature to be found in the Bible. The book of Job is as different from Judges as either is from the Psalms. Some interpreters suggest that the biblical documents present a progressive revelation of God, on the whole revealing his true character more clearly in later documents than in earlier ones. There is no question that there is a great diversity of religious content to be found throughout the pages of the Bible. Assuming otherwise can lead to problems of interpretation, and more serious theological problems. And at some points, seeing through the apparent problems for divine goodness is just a matter of proper translation. Those passages in which the King James Version has God saying he is responsible for "evil" are better and more recently translated as involving "calamity" or "disaster." That which appears evil, or that which involves calamity, disaster or suffering perceived by the sufferer as evil may not be, all things considered, evil at all. Punishment, for example, may sometimes be morally justified. Thus it has been judged by most Christians throughout the centuries that, despite any appearances to the contrary, it is a central biblical theme that God is wholly good.

More controversial, at least nowadays, is the stronger claim that God is necessarily good, our thesis (2). This is a modal claim about God's character. Modality, or any modal claim, has to do with such notions as necessity, impossibility and possibility. There are many contemporary philosophical controversies over various matters of modality, and the controversy over the necessity of God's goodness is just one of these. But before we can appreciate fully the nature of this particular controversy, as well as its potential resolution, we need to note briefly three different ways in which divine goodness has been understood. Taking up a bit of quasiscientific terminology, we can refer to these three structural representations of God's goodness as *three models of divine goodness*.

The *plenitude of being model* explicates that aspect of divine goodness which is distinctively metaphysical. According to this model, to say that God is good and to insist further that God is perfectly good is to hold that God is metaphysically, or ontologically, complete, without flaw, defect or lack with respect to his *being*. God, on this model, is the fullness of being in two respects. First, he himself exemplifies perfection in the Anselmian sense. And secondly, he is the metaphysical source of all being and thus of all other goodness.

The plenitude of being model explains God's goodness in terms of what he *is*. The other two models explain it in terms of what he *does*. The former focuses on the nature of his existence, the latter zero in on the nature of his actions. According to the *duty model*, God acts in perfect accordance with all those principles which specify moral duties. He is, for example, a perfect promise-keeper and a perfect truth-teller, as well as being the greatest possible respecter of persons. This model tells us that anything which *ought to be done* by a free moral agent in God's relevant circumstances is *perfectly done* by God without fail. God never acts in a way contrary to true moral principles.

The *benevolence model* tells us that God does not do only that which would be morally required of a moral agent in his circumstances, but that he goes beyond the call of duty, graciously and benevolently doing good that need not have been done. He brings into existence good which is not merited, deserved, required, obligated or necessitated. Such is his gracious goodness.

These three models each capture some important respect in which God is believed by Christians to be good. They are appropriately thought of as complementing one another in such a way as to spell out together the complexity of what can be meant when it is said quite simply that God is good, wholly and completely good. Yet when theists go on to say that God is necessarily good, some philosophers believe that this strong claim, together with one of our three models, creates a troubling philosophical problem. In order to understand the full impact of that problem, we first must examine the grounds on which many theologians and philosophers have claimed that God is necessarily good.

The Necessity of God's Goodness

In the New Testament, the epistle of James tells us that "God cannot be tempted by evil" (Jas 1:13). Most of the great theists of the past have assured us that this is because God cannot do evil. His goodness is not fragile, vulnerable to temptation or lapse. He is necessarily a doer of the good. His will is thus dependably set in the direction of the morally excellent. Many theists have affirmed this, and a number have thought that it can be proved.

The following argument, for example, is suggested by a passage in the writings of St. Thomas Aquinas (A.D. 1225-1274):[3]

(1) Agents can do only what they see as good.

(2) To see evil as a good is to be in error.

(3) God cannot be in error.

So

(4) God cannot see evil as a good. (2, 3)

And thus

5) God cannot do evil. (1, 4)

To evaluate an argument such as this one, we need to ask whether it is valid and whether its premises are all true. An argument is *valid* when it is such that, necessarily, if its premises are all true then so is its conclusion. A valid argument is truth-conveying. Its structure is such as to convey truth reliably from premises to conclusion. Reflection can show that the argument we have in our sights is valid. That is to say, if its premises are all true, then we are guaranteed that so is its conclusion. But we must now ask about whether its premises are all true. A valid argument with all true premises is called a *sound* argument. So by investigating each of this argument's premises, we are now seeking to determine its *soundness,* having already seen its *validity.*

Line (5) of the argument is inferred (as noted) from lines (1) and (4). But line (4) is endorsed only through having been inferred from lines (2) and (3). So it is only lines (1), (2) and (3) which are the basic premises of the argument. Let's look at them in reverse order.

Premise (3) would be endorsed by most theists regardless of their beliefs about the modality of divine goodness. It seems to follow straightforwardly from the traditional belief that God is essentially omniscient, i.e., that God by nature enjoys perfect knowledge. So, from a traditional point of view, line (3) does not seem in any way to be an objectionable claim about God. Premise (2) can be taken to be just as unobjectionable, rooted as it also is in apparent conceptual truths about good and evil. It is only with respect to premise (1) that serious questions have been raised.

This premise is based on a theory of morality deriving from Plato, according to which wrongdoing is always, inevitably, a matter of ignorance. On this view, we are inexorably drawn to what we see as good, or judge to be good. So, bad action only comes from bad judgment, in the sense of false belief. If I rob a bank, I must have decided that, given my circumstances, it is a good thing for me to get the bank's money and, in the situation, good to get it in this way (whatever the motivation). Otherwise, I wouldn't perform the robbery. I can do only what I see, at least *at the time,* as good. This is the view behind premise (1).

Critics have been quick to point out that, for any object of action *x,* it is one thing to judge that *x* is good, another altogether to judge that *x* is good *for me.* If I rob a bank, it may be that I must have judged that to be good *for me* to do at the time; it doesn't follow at all that I thereby must have judged it to be good *in a moral sense*. To think of something as convenient or advantageous is not the same thing as thinking it to be morally good. So even if it could be shown to be a psychological truth that agents can do only what they see as good *for themselves*, which is the most that standard examples show, it would not follow that premise (1) is a truth about distinctively moral good. And, as a matter of fact, we can't even get as far as

(1') Agents can do only what they see as good *for themselves*

because even this claim seems to restrict unduly the possible sources of wrongdoing to just ignorance. And it seems that people go wrong from uncontrollable, or at least uncontrolled, impulse as well as from ignorance about the relevant moral facts. That is to say, it seems that irrational forces often incline us to evil even when we are aware of the immorality of what we do, and even when we have not formed a judgment that, all things considered, the act, though morally evil, is nonetheless in some sense good for us. But if impulse is a source of evil, and the Thomistic argument we have been considering does not block it from ever being operative in the case of God, the argument cannot produce for us the conclusion that God cannot do evil.

In a recent book R. G. Swinburne recognizes that evil can be done from impulse as well as ignorance and argues that since God is both omniscient and *perfectly free*—that is, subject to no irrational forces—we can after all conclude that he cannot possibly do evil.[4] If ignorance and impulse are the only two possible sources of evil, and Swinburne has succeeded in showing that God is vulnerable to neither, then we do have the desired conclusion that God cannot do evil produced from independently plausible theistic beliefs.

A person who is free in a radical sense, however, is not just free from compulsion or impulsion. He is free to act as he chooses, whether he has a reason to so act or not. It seems that a truly free being is free to make arbitrary choices, and is free to make even perverse choices. If I am not impelled by irrational forces to perform a certain act *A*, realize that *A* is wrong, but just do *A* anyway, I can be said to act perversely. Perversity seems to be one of the (less attractive) options available to a radically free being. It is available to us imperfectly free humans, so it can be natural to think it would be available to a perfectly free God. If not, Swinburne has offered us no reason to think not. He says nothing to rule out this apparent third possible source of evil-doing from ever being operative in the life of God. Because of this, his argument also fails to produce the desired conclusion that God cannot possibly do evil. And furthermore, it is difficult to see how any additional strengthening of this general type of argument could possibly attain the desired result.

A strategy deriving from the great medieval philosopher William of Ockham (c. A.D. 1285-1349) would take an entirely different tack. To put it as simply as possible, this argument begins by submitting that 'good' is to be defined as 'whatever God wills.' Thus

(A) God does good

and

(B) God does whatever God wills

express the same proposition. But (B) obviously expresses a necessary truth (derived from the quite general conceptual truth about the action of any omnipotent, omniscient being that no such being can be prevented from doing anything he wills to do). So (A) must express a necessary truth. But if it is necessarily true that God does good, it is impossible that God does evil. Whatever he does is, by definition, good. Thus, God cannot do evil. We have vindicated the conviction that divine goodness has the high status of necessity and have done so quite simply.

Or have we? We have here an argument from a definition, and an argument that moves from premise to conclusion very quickly. Too quickly, according to most critics. We seem to have slipped here into what nonphilosophers like to call "mere semantics." Ockham has tailored a definition of 'good' to suit his purposes and, like pulling a rabbit from a hat, has produced the conclusion he desired. We cannot just define a certain strength of character into existence.

First, we should take care to appreciate what can push someone in the direction of this Ockhamist argument. Are we to define 'good' totally independently of anything having to do with God? Is goodness independent of God? Surely not, many theists have insisted. If there were a standard of goodness independent of God, it would be a standard he would have to measure up to, a standard against which he could be judged. But then such a standard would seem to be higher than God, more ultimate than deity in our world view, and this is clearly unacceptable for any traditional theist who wants to maintain an exalted conception of God.

As we shall see in our chapter on creation, however, there can be standards of goodness conceptually distinguishable from God's will, or the content of what God wills, without its following that these standards are independent of God or somehow more ultimate than God. Thus, to retain a properly exalted conception of God, we need not think we should adopt the Ockhamistic strategy of defining 'good' as 'whatever God wills' in the first place.

And that's a good thing, because Ockham's strategy and resulting argument suffer from one debilitating problem: they establish the necessity of God's goodness only at the price of evacuating the claim that God is good of all its rich, determinate meaning. Let us call this the *vacuity objection*. The vacuity objection first points out that most of us, when we call a person good in anything like a moral sense, mean to say that the person is, for example, a truth-teller and a promise-keeper. And this is a quite determinate characterization of a person. If we accept the Ockhamistic definition of 'good,' then to say of a human being that he is good is only to say of him that he does whatever God wills. Unless we also know what it is that God wills, the claim that a man is good will have much less content to it than the more determinate content most of us typically take it to have. And when applied to God, 'good' would lose all its determinate content whatsoever. 'God is good' would then be a vacuous statement and not the tremendously important substantive claim most of us take it to be. Its truth would be compatible with the claim that God is also sadistically cruel and a chronic liar. And that is utterly outrageous. Thus, the strategy suggested in the Ockhamistic argument exacts far too high a price for what it then makes an empty modal assurance about God.[5]

The arguments suggested by Aquinas, Swinburne and Ockham all seem to fail. And many other arguments have been attempted for the view that God is necessarily good which seem to attain just as little success.[6] Why then have so many theists endorsed the belief that God is necessarily, or essentially, good? I believe that for a great many Christian philosophers and theologians, this conviction has not come as the result of an elaborate argument or proof at all, but that it is simply the result of an intuitive judgment that it would be better for God to be utterly invulnerable to evil than to be capable of wickedness. It is simply an Anselmian intuition that underlies most theists' endorsement of this belief. The highest form of perfection requires the impossibility of evil-doing on the part of the perfect being. Thus the necessity of God's goodness is a deliverance of perfect being theology, and does not stand in any obvious need of independent argument.

The Problems of Praiseworthiness and Moral Freedom

The conviction that God is necessarily good seems very important to those who endorse it. But critics have been quick to point out that it leads to problems. Consider first what we can call the *problem of praiseworthiness*, as expressed in the following argument:

(1) A person is praiseworthy for an action only if he could have refrained from performing it.

(2) A necessarily good being cannot refrain from performing good actions.

So

(3) A necessarily good being is not praiseworthy for any of his good actions.

If

(4) God is necessarily good,

then

(5) God is not praiseworthy for any of his good actions.

But, surely

(6) God is praiseworthy for his good actions.

So

(7) It is not the case that God is necessarily good.

All theists hold God to be worthy of praise. So any argument such as this which purports to move from considerations about praiseworthiness to a conclusion that God does not exemplify goodness with the high modal status of necessity must be taken seriously indeed.

We have here a valid argument form. But is the argument sound? Backtracking through the steps of the argument, we find three basic premises, lines (1), (2) and (6). Line (6) just expresses the universal theistic view that God is in fact praiseworthy. As the psalmist says:

Great is the LORD, and greatly to be praised. (Ps 48:1)

For Christians, this is a non-negotiable aspect of our conception of God. So we must scrutinize lines (1) and (2) to evaluate the force of this argument.

The first premise presents a certain requirement for praiseworthiness, a requirement of freedom. In the same way that we do not blame a person for an action which was literally forced upon him, it seems that we do not typically praise a person for an action he could not possibly have avoided. Praising and blaming actions, or, to be more precise, praising and blaming agents for their actions, thus seems to presuppose that there were alternatives to those actions open to their agents. As we do not thank an electronically controlled door for opening in our path, we do not praise a person for something that was forced upon him. Freedom does seem to be a condition of praiseworthiness.

But does premise (1) indeed succeed in capturing precisely what that freedom must involve? It is possible to have doubts here. For an agent is praiseworthy for a good act he performs just in case (a) he intended to perform it, and (b) no causal conditions independent of his own character and decisions alone forced the action upon him, or rendered him such that he was unable to avoid it. To be responsible for his act, the agent must be free from external compulsion. Typically, in human experience, the holding true of condition (b), the freedom from external compulsion, is manifested in there being real alternative courses of action equally available to the agent. But consider a case involving God. Suppose that, in a particular situation, there is a best possible action God can perform and that, due to his necessary goodness, it is necessarily the case that in this situation he will perform that action. Now, we are thinking of God's necessary goodness as an aspect of his own eternal character. If the necessity of his action in this situation just arises out of that feature of his character, we have no reason to think of it as having been forced on him by causal conditions independent of his character and decisions. If he performs it intentionally, and no such external causal conditions compelled his performance, then it is quite reasonable to hold that he was responsible for it, and thus praiseworthy in reference to it, contrary to what premise (1) demands. But even apart from these doubts about premise (1), the argument we are examining can be judged a failure on account of its second step.

Premise (2) seems to be just an explication of what it means to be necessarily good. And surely it is true that a necessarily good being cannot refrain from performing good actions, in the sense that he cannot refrain from ever performing any good actions whatsoever. But the apparent effectiveness of premise (2) in the argument here is due entirely to the fact that it trades on an ambiguity. (2) can mean either

(2') A necessarily good being cannot refrain from ever performing any good actions whatsoever,

which is true, but will not produce the conclusion of the argument, or

(2″) A necessarily good being cannot refrain from performing any of the good actions he performs,

which is the interpretation needed for the argument to go through. But this, unfortunately for the argument, and fortunately for the Anselmian theist, expresses a proposition that is false and thus yields an unsound overall argument. A necessarily good being cannot perform any evil actions. But it is compatible with being necessarily good that a being have the option to perform or refrain from performing any number of good actions which are not required of him, but which rather fall into the category of the *supererogatory*. An act is supererogatory if it is good, but not obligatory. A supererogatory act is one which goes beyond the call of duty, as it is often said. And clearly most theists believe that God does many good things which are not required or obligatory but which he does freely out of his gracious love, as the benevolence model of divine goodness suggests. For all of these, and for good which results from them, a necessarily good God is worthy of praise. Thus, what can appear at first glance to be a powerful objection against the claim that God is necessarily good dissipates under a more attentive scrutiny.

There is, however, another related problem which has been thought to attend the conviction that God is necessarily good. We can call it the *problem of moral freedom.* Put quite simply, the problem is this: Being a moral agent, a person capable of and engaging in morally assessable conduct, requires having a certain sort of freedom with respect to one's actions. A being who is not free in the requisite sense does not perform actions which are morally characterizable at all, as either morally good or morally bad. A standard analysis of the conditions for moral agency often known as *libertarianism* specifies that *morally significant freedom,* the sort of freedom required for full moral agency, is the freedom to have done "morally otherwise" than as one in fact does. If I perform a bad action with morally significant freedom, then I could have performed a morally good action instead, and I am morally accountable for what I in fact do. But if God is necessarily good, he has no alternatives available to him apart from doing what is right. He is, in particular, never free to do evil. But if that is so, then he lacks morally significant freedom. And if he is not morally free, then we must conclude that, contrary to what we might have thought, he is not a moral agent at all, and his goodness, whatever it is, is not moral goodness.

The problem can be summed up like this: "necessary moral goodness" is a contradiction in terms. If something is necessitated, it can't be morally good; and if something is morally good, it can't be necessitated. Thus, holding that God's goodness is necessary prevents us from holding that God is morally good.

This strikes most people as a shocking and unorthodox conclusion. But things are not quite as simple as this conclusion makes them look. We need to consider the relation between God and morality a bit more closely before we can properly evaluate this conclusion, and thus the argument which has led to it. I believe that this version of the problem of moral freedom has caused many people to give up, for no good reason, the belief that God's goodness is necessary, in order to save the view that his goodness is moral.

Suppose God promises Moses to help him lead his people out of Egypt. Moses trusts God and makes bold to approach Pharaoh. When the time comes for action, is God free to give Moses assistance or to refrain from helping at all? Is he free to keep *or* break his promise? Does he have any options? Well, if God has given Moses his word that he will help, and he is necessarily good, it is strictly impossible that, when the time for action comes, God will renege. At that time, he has no freedom not to help. But if that is the case, then God's giving of assistance to Moses at that time is not a case of morally assessable promise-keeping. And, more generally, if God necessarily acts in accordance with all those principles which would specify duties for moral agents in his relevant circumstances, he is never free to act in dereliction of a duty. But a being who cannot possibly violate a duty cannot possibly have duties. For only a moral agent with morally significant freedom is the kind of being to whom duties apply. Therefore, if God is necessarily good in the manner specified, he cannot literally have duties.

But what of the duty model of divine goodness? If God cannot have duties, is the duty model nullified? The answer, somewhat surprisingly, is no. The duty model of divine goodness does not consist in the claim that God *has* duties. It says only that his activity can be modeled on the conduct of an idealized moral agent who in the relevant circumstances does have duties and satisfies them perfectly.

Many philosophers have drawn an important distinction between following a rule and merely acting in accordance with a rule. Behavior which results from obeying a rule can be distinguished logically from behavior which accords with the rule but does not result from an attempt to obey it, even though the two forms of conduct may be empirically indistinguishable to an observer. Something similar to this distinction can help us to understand the relation between God and moral duties, and thus the legitimate application of the duty model to God.

We can hold that moral principles which function as *prescriptive* or *proscriptive* for human conduct stand in some other relation to divine conduct. We can even go so far as to claim that they are merely *descriptive* of the shape of divine activity. But the important difference is as follows: We human beings, imperfect and weak as we are, exist in a state of being *bound* by moral duty. In this state, we act under obligation, either satisfying or contravening our duties. Because of his distinctive nature, God does not share our ontological status. Specifically, he does not share our relation to moral principles—that of being bound by some of these principles as duties. Nevertheless, God acts perfectly in accordance with those principles which would express duties for a moral agent in his relevant circumstances. And he does so necessarily. So although God does not literally have any duties on this construal of the duty model, we can still have well-grounded expectations concerning divine conduct by knowing those principles which would govern the conduct of a perfect, duty-bound moral agent who acted as in fact God does. We understand and anticipate God's activity by analogy with the behavior of a completely good moral agent.

So, is God's goodness only analogous to moral goodness but not itself in any way an example of moral goodness? I think this would be too extreme a conclusion. For consider the benevolence model of divine goodness. According to it, God's goodness consists, in part, in his disposition toward gracious acts of loving supererogation. He does particular instances of good which no moral principle indicates ought to be done. If he makes Moses a promise, he is not free to break the promise. But why did he make the promise in the first place? Was that a necessity of some sort? Surely there are cases where the good engaged in by God is purely a result of his grace. And any particular such good is one God could have refrained from bringing about. In supererogation, God does exercise the freedom of alternatives sufficient, I think, to render that action properly moral action.

But if our application of the duty model to God does not itself ascribe moral goodness to God, does the duty model nonetheless represent any kind of literal goodness? In what sense of 'goodness' could it? Unlike that presented by the plenitude of being model, it is not exactly metaphysical goodness. But because of the freedom required of moral goodness, it is not exactly moral goodness either. The benevolence model can be said to capture the moral goodness of God, the plenitude of being model, his metaphysical or ontological goodness. It is possible to treat both these sorts of goodness as species of a broader category of what we might call "axiological goodness" (from the Greek *axia*, "value"). To shed light on our problem it will be helpful to identify a further, midlevel category of goodness, contained within the overarching category of axiological goodness and containing the category of moral goodness. We can think of it as the broadest category of goodness consisting in what an agent does or is disposed to do. We can call this form of goodness *volitional goodness* (from the Latin *volo,* "I will"). Volitional goodness can be thought of as goodness residing in or arising out of a being's will or character when that will or character is not itself causally determined in that respect by anything independent of that being.

To be an agent, such as a human being, who gladly engages in deeds of supererogation and freely acts in accordance with moral principles, satisfying moral duties, is to be in a state of volitional, and thus axiological, goodness. To be an agent such as God who freely engages in acts of grace, or supererogation, but necessarily acts in accordance with moral principles, is to be in the greatest possible state of volitional goodness. It may be held that for human beings, at least in this life, volitional goodness and moral goodness coincide. For God, however, one form of moral goodness, supererogation, is a component of his volitional goodness; whereas another aspect of his volitional goodness is his necessarily acting in accordance with moral principles—not literally a form of moral goodness at all on the standard libertarian analysis of the conditions for morality, but on this view a contributing element or aspect of divine volitional, and thus axiological, goodness.

On this view, God's intentionally acting in accordance with what for us are moral principles specifying duties would be sufficient, given his nature and ontological status, for that conduct to count as good, not morally but volitionally, and thus axiologically. Axiological agency need not be thought of as logically incompatible, on every ontological level, with all forms of necessitation. It could thus be reasonable for the Anselmian theist to hold that a form of necessitation is compatible with—indeed, a condition of—God's being a perfectly good axiological agent, a greater than which is not possible.

With these distinctions in hand, we can say that an analogical employment of the duty model is indeed a partial explication of divine goodness. Part of God's goodness does consist in his acting in perfect accord with those principles which would provide duties for a lesser being. This use of the model would then be an explication, not of God's moral goodness, but of his volitional and thus, more generally, axiological goodness. When religious people claim that God is morally good, meaning that he acts in accord with moral principles, they are merely using that axiological conception with which they are most familiar, moral goodness, to describe or model an aspect of divinity functionally isomorphic with, though ontologically different from, human goodness.

But some philosophers will protest that if God's life lacks any single component at all of standard, straightforward, literal *moral* goodness, then, contrary to the requirements of perfect being theology, God is not after all a greatest possible and worship-worthy being. The reasoning seems to be something like this: If it is a good thing for moral goodness to exist, it is surely an intrinsic good. But if this is so, then in addition any component or condition of moral goodness, such as the having of full, morally significant freedom or the having of duties one satisfies, is itself an intrinsic good. In other words, all those properties which allow for, or constitute, ordinary moral goodness are great-making properties. But the lack of any such great-making property, the argument goes, will result in an individual's having some status less than that of a greatest possible being.

On the picture of divine goodness I am suggesting, there is not to be found within the distinctively divine life of God a hard-fought achievement of moral duty fulfillment. This component of moral goodness is absent. Nor is there full, morally significant freedom. On this view, God does not nobly refuse to avail himself of evil options open to him. He does not have that sort of choice. But it can be argued then that in my attempt to expound and defend what initially can seem to be an exalted idea of God, I have unwittingly arrived instead at an unworthy conception of divinity.

Once, in expressing a mock sense of superiority to George Washington, Mark Twain quipped:

George Washington could not tell a lie.

I *can* tell a lie but won't.

The attitude expressed here seems to be the one, or at least closely related to the one, generating this line of criticism: It is better to be triumphant in moral freedom than to be necessarily good, unable to do evil. But is this so? If the necessity comes from outside oneself, that is one thing. If the necessity is merely a reflection of one's nature, as in the case of God, that is very different.

First, it should be said that even if having full, morally significant freedom and thus having moral duties, is a great-making property, and one which, on the view of God as necessarily good, God does not have, it does not follow that he is less than perfect, contrary to the requirements of perfect being theology. All that perfect being theology requires is that God have the greatest possible array of *compossible* great-making properties, not that he have all great-making properties. And if being necessarily good and having duties are both great-making properties, then they are obviously not compossible great-making properties—they cannot be had together. Thus, lacking one of them is not necessarily incompatible with being a greatest possible being.

And there is every reason to suppose that the property of having a hard-won moral goodness, or the property of having duties is the sort of property a perfect being can do without. Any such property is a good thing, but it may be a good for only a certain kind of being, the kind vulnerable to evil, the kind of being we humans are. And the property of having morally significant freedom—being able to go wrong as well as right—can plausibly be thought to be not an excellence of the highest order, but rather an imperfection, in contrast with the divine standard. This judgment is at least as plausible as a judgment to the contrary and is, I think, sufficient to show that the typical Anselmian conviction that God is necessarily good need not be thought to fall to this criticism. The exalted view of God it seems to be, it is. God's goodness can be thought of as complete and as stable in the strongest possible sense.

4

The Power of God

*I*n the book of Jeremiah, the prophet reports that in one prayer to God he said:

Ah, Lord GOD! Behold, Thou has made the heavens and the earth by Thy great power and by Thine outstretched arm! Nothing is too difficult for Thee. (Jer 32:17)

He also recounts that God answered his prayer, saying,

Behold, I am the LORD, the God of all flesh; is anything too difficult for Me? (Jer 32:27)

In the circumstances, the point about God's power obviously bore repeating. The absoluteness of that power is an important theme in the Old Testament and into the New, where Jesus is quoted as having said that

with God all things are possible. (Mt 19:26)

The religious importance of this theme is impossible to overestimate. In both testaments, God is believed to have made his people certain promises, grand promises concerning eternity. If he is perfectly good, we know he will endeavor to keep those promises. But unless he is sufficiently powerful, we cannot be confident that he will succeed. To think of God as creator of our world, though, is to think of him as having immense power on an almost inconceivable scale. To think of him as the greatest possible being is to think of that power as perfect. And the greatest possible power can surely sustain the grandest imaginable promises. Thus we can see that the theistic attempt to understand the magnitude or scope of God's power is far from being just an exercise in speculative theorizing. It is connected up with vital human religious concerns which affect the way we think of ourselves and our future.

The Magnitude of Divine Power

Picking up on many passages in the Bible, Christians throughout the centuries have characterized God as "almighty" and "all-powerful." Philosophers and theologians have sought to register the magnitude of divine power by saying that God is *omnipotent*. They have also put a great deal of effort into trying to explain precisely what this means. What exactly is it to be perfectly powerful?

Philosophers have explored two ways of explicating the concept of omnipotence. There is first of all, and most commonly, the attempt to specify the magnitude of omnipotence by indicating the range of things an omnipotent being can do—the range of acts he can perform, tasks he can accomplish, or states of affairs he can bring about. This sort of analysis usually begins with the simple, commonplace religious assertion that:

(1) God can do everything,

and proceeds to test its initially unrestricted universality ("everything") against various logical, metaphysical and theological intuitions which seem to call for more cautious qualification. For example, it is often pointed out that if "everything" is meant to encompass the logically impossible as well as the logically possible, then (1) entails that God can create spherical cubes, and married bachelors, as well as bring about states of affairs in which he both does and does not exist at one and the same time. But to say that God is so powerful that he can do the logically impossible is not pious or reverential; it is just confused. For logically impossible tasks are not just particularly esoteric and unusually difficult tasks—when you have attempted to describe an act or task and end up with the expression of a logical impossibility, you end up with nothing that can even be a candidate for power ascriptions. To put it vividly, in many such descriptions we can say that one half of the description just cancels the other half out, and vice versa. For instance, if we ask God to create a "married bachelor," each of the two terms cancels the other out. It is as if we were to write something down and then immediately erase it—the net result being nothing at all, no task specified. Now, not all impossibility can be thought of in even roughly this way. But the general point is that if we insist that God can do the logically impossible, we find that if we were to attempt to describe the results of his so doing, we violate the conditions under which, and under which alone, we are able to engage in coherent discourse capable of describing reality. So, most philosophers suggest that (1) be qualified accordingly, resulting in something like:

(2) God can do everything logically possible,

which is still quite an extraordinary claim. For the rest of us, there is a tremendous disparity between what is logically possible and what we can do. For God, (2) tells us, there is no such gap.

But even (2) seems insufficiently cautious, many philosophers have urged. For, assuming that each of us has free will, it is logically possible for us to do something not done by God. But we do not want to say that God can do something not done by God. That is to say, we do not want to commit ourselves to holding, because of what (2) stipulates, that God could possibly do something which would be such that, once done, it would properly bear the description "Not done by God." This, again, is just confused. So perhaps we need to be a little more careful still and express the range of God's power by saying that:

(3) Anything which it is logically possible for God to do, he can do.

And this is a phrasing which does not commit us to holding that God can do things "not done by God," or make things not made by God. It is impossible that God make a table thereafter properly described as "Not made by God," and so (3) does not locate such a task within the range of divine omnipotence. But (3) still expresses an extraordinary conception of divine power. It is logically possible for me to bench-press eight hundred pounds, but I can't do it. There is a tremendous disparity between what is logically possible *for me* and what is in my power. And (3) assures us that there is no such disparity faced by God.

But certain features of (3) can still be seen as problematic. The content of (3) leaves open the possibility that God could be by nature weak in numerous ways, that he could be such that many basic tasks are impossible for him, and yet by the conditions expressed in (3) still qualify as omnipotent. Any weakness that was essential to God, such that overcoming it would be logically impossible for him, would be compatible with calling him omnipotent. But do we want to allow this? Surely, some further rephrasing is called for. Perhaps:

(4) Anything that it is logically possible for a perfect being to do, God can do

would solve our problems. For any weakness is surely an imperfection. And an essential weakness would be an even greater imperfection. (4), accordingly, does not allow what (3) would seem to allow, namely, the compatibility between essential weaknesses and omnipotence.

The informativeness of (4), however, depends on our having some prior sense of what it is logically possible for a perfect being to do. And if part of perfection is omnipotence, we seem to confront here a sort of circularity that should at least give us pause. The philosopher Peter Geach once concluded that this avenue of searching for an adequate account of the magnitude of divine power is a dead end, and stated:

> When people have tried to read into 'God can do everything' a signification not of Pious Intention but of Philosophical Truth, they have only landed themselves in intractable problems and hopeless confusions; no graspable sense has ever been given to this sentence that did not lead to self-contradiction or at least to conclusions manifestly untenable from the Christian point of view.[1]

Geach's recommendation was to give up the ascription of omnipotence to God and to characterize him instead as "almighty," a word Geach reserved to mean "having power *over* all things." In other words, Geach believed it was hopeless to try to understand God's power in terms of things God can do, which he took to be the only way of explicating omnipotence, and so he attempted to distinguish conceptually a different way of understanding divine power altogether, which he labeled 'almightiness.' Not many philosophers have followed Geach in his abandonment of the concept of omnipotence, but it must be said that those who have persevered along the lines we have explored have found themselves faced with increasing complexity.[2] There is an alternative, however. We can seek to explore the notion of omnipotence not in terms of the range of *things God can do*, but a bit more abstractly, and at the same time, at least potentially, more simply, in terms of *powers God possesses.*

The idea of a power is a very basic, fundamental idea. It is such a basic idea that it is very difficult to analyze or explain, since analysis and explanation typically break up the complex into the simple, or illuminate the unfamiliar by reference to the familiar. We normally give an account of one idea by explaining it in terms of more basic ideas. But the idea of a power is so basic in our conceptualization of the world that it is hard to find much to say in elucidation of it. But we can say a few things that are helpful for getting our bearings.

Our first acquaintance with power is, presumably, our experience of the power of personal agency. Other people act upon us, and we act upon them, as well as upon the world around us. When a small child wants a toy, he reaches for it and moves it closer to where he sits. He has exercised his power upon the world around him to get what he wants, to effect the satisfaction of his desires. He finds that he does not just have desires caused in him by things in the world; he finds that he himself can form intentions and cause changes in the world in response to those desires. He experiences, in his own small way, power—causal power.

This is arguably the most fundamental, or at least is closely related to the most fundamental, kind of power. The most fundamental sort of power, in the sense of ultimacy, would be the power to create *ex nihilo* ("from nothing"), the sheer power to bring into existence things which are not brought into being merely by the arrangement of previously existing things. Some philosophers categorize this as a kind of causal power—the power to cause being. Others divide the conceptual terrain a bit differently, and think of causal power as power which can only be exercised upon previously existing things, in accordance with causal laws which are already in place. Regardless of whether creative and causal power are distinguished as basically different kinds of power, or whether the former is treated as just the ultimate instance of the latter, both are metaphysical forms of power and are thus relevant to our understanding of the power of God.

In this regard, creative and causal power are to be distinguished from what we refer to as "political power" and "legal power." When we talk of political power we often mean to refer to no more than the entrenchment or institutionalization of personal influence or group influence with respect to matters of political governance. In legal matters, the power of attorney is just an authority, duly conferred upon one, to act for another person in business dealings or kindred actions. Political and legal power are powers defined in terms of, and dependent upon, previously existing rules or practices forming human social activity. If I am not a participant rightly placed in the appropriate practices or institutions, I cannot be said to have various powers of this sort. As God is not a creature participating in such creaturely institutions, he is not said to have power in these senses, but rather always in the more fundamental metaphysical sense.

Some further distinctions can be drawn to help us better understand the role of causal power in our conceptualization of the world. In our thought and talk about the world, we often attribute power, or the lack of certain powers, to objects and people. We often say what someone "can" or "cannot" do, and we sometimes assume that such talk always can be translated into talk about powers. But if I say of some task x that Jones cannot do x, I do not necessarily ascribe to Jones any lack of power at all. The little word 'can' can serve many different functions; the word 'cannot' cannot always be assumed to mean the same thing. Can-locutions sometimes attribute power. Often they do not. Likewise, cannot-locutions sometimes attribute lack of power. But often they do not. When I say "Jones cannot do x," I may mean that Jones lacks the *power* necessary for doing x. Or I may think he has the power, but lacks the *skill* requisite for using that power to do x. Or, again, I may grant him the power and the skill, but believe that he lacks the *opportunity* for drawing on that power, by means of that skill, in the circumstances in which he finds himself. But even with all the requisite power, skill and opportunity, poor Jones may lack the *practical knowledge* of his situation—of his power, skill and opportunity, as well as of how they could come together for the performance of *x*—necessary for the doing of *x*. And it may be *this* lack I mean to convey, or which I have in mind, when I say "Jones cannot do *x*."

One other distinction can be drawn here, one relating to questions of moral character. Suppose that a young boy with a precociously obnoxious personality and a proclivity to mischief lives down the street from old Jones. He bothers Jones daily in extremely irritating ways. A neighbor who witnesses this regular harassment comments to a mutual friend, "If I were Jones, I'd throttle the kid. Why doesn't he just catch him, wrap his hands around that loud, whiny windpipe, and give it a good long squeeze?" The friend might reply, "Jones could not possibly do anything like that. He's not capable of such behavior." The friend need not be attributing to Jones any lack of physical power, skill, opportunity or practical knowledge here. In fact, he's probably not. Often, when we say that a certain person is not "capable" of a morally dubious or improper line of action, what we mean to indicate is that doing such a thing would be contrary to a firmly entrenched character that person has, that the desire or inclination to perform the action is not within the range of his possible desires and inclinations, or that a serious intention to engage in the action is prohibited by a stable moral stance characteristic of that person. And this is a very different matter from anything having to do with power, skill, opportunity or practical knowledge. We can somewhat stipulatively refer to this matter as a consideration of "moral capability," or just *capability*, to set it apart from the other factors we have identified as determinative with respect to what a person can or cannot do.

We can think of power, skill, opportunity and practical knowledge as comprising one cluster of factors concerning what an individual can or cannot do, and capability as defining the moral dimension relevant to this. But there is often one final factor potentially involved in action, and it is difficult to know whether to classify it with the larger cluster of factors which we can refer to as "the ability-cluster," or rather with the moral dimension of capability. What

I have in mind is often called "will power," and is just the element of determination or persistence in pursuing a line of action which takes either time or effort to attain or complete. A person may have the requisite ability-cluster, as already identified, for *x,* and it may be that doing *x* is consistent with the person's settled values, but the individual cannot do *x* because of a lack of will power or determination. This can be viewed as something more akin to a lack of power, or as something more like a moral weakness. Perhaps we can allot to it an intermediate status, as in the diagram:

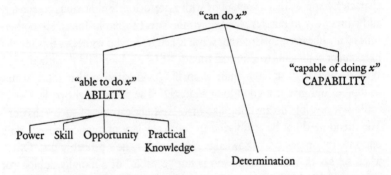

Our informal, colloquial uses of 'can' and 'cannot' irregularly convey many different things. They do not always convey convictions about power. We can understand the conceptual terrain that our idea of power in the metaphysical sense is meant to cover only if we keep it distinct from these other many different ideas with which it is often confused when we talk simply of what an individual can or cannot do. This, in part, is what makes any explication of omnipotence in terms of what God can do such a complicated business. And it is this which, when kept in mind, will help us to understand and defend the simpler conception of omnipotence in terms of powers possessed.

So, what is the magnitude of divine power? In his book *The God of the Philosophers,* Anthony Kenny says:

A being is omnipotent if it has every power which it is logically possible to possess.[3]

He goes on to explain:

It is logically possible to possess a power, I suggest, if the exercise of the power does not *as such* involve any logical impossibility.[4]

And he further specifies that by this, he means that:

> . . . there is no incoherence in the description of what it is to exercise that power. For a power to be a logically possible power, it is not necessary that every exercise of it should be coherently conceivable, but only that some exercise of it should be.

Along these lines, it can be said that when we describe God as omnipotent, we commit ourselves to his having every power which it is logically possible to possess. This is a very simple account of omnipotence, and seems clearly to present a view sufficiently exalted to accord with the perspective of perfect being theology. Indeed, it is a view which looks tailor-made for this perspective, for it is impossible to imagine coherently any greater account of perfect power.

Problems for Divine Power

Many critics of theism have alleged that calling God omnipotent, or perfect in power, lands the theist in a number of difficult philosophical problems. One particularly renowned problem is known as "the paradox of the stone." Somewhat akin to the form of argument known as the *reductio ad absurdum* ("reduction to absurdity"), the stone paradox arises in the asking and answering of a question. With this question-and-answer dynamic, the critic is trying to show that the ascription of omnipotence to God is self-defeating, or that the notion itself of omnipotence is incoherent.

The question is this: If God is omnipotent, then can he create a stone which he cannot lift (cause to rise)? If the answer is 'no' then, the critic reasons, there is something God cannot do, namely, create the sort of stone in question, and so he is not, after all, omnipotent. If the answer is 'yes', he can create such a stone, then again there is a task he cannot perform, namely, lift the stone once created, and therefore again he is not omnipotent. Regardless of which answer is given to the question, the conclusion follows that God is not omnipotent. But we were assuming that he is. So the supposition that God is omnipotent must be ultimately self-defeating or incoherent. Therefore, there cannot be such a being. This is the critic's argument.

First, it should be noted that the critic is assuming throughout that if there is something specifiable that God cannot do, it follows that he lacks omnipotence. But if omnipotence is understood as perfect power along the lines suggested by Kenny, this is too quick an inference. For if it is true to say with respect to some particular act-description that God cannot perform the sort of act described, then it seems to follow only that God lacks either the power, the skill, the opportunity, the determination or the moral capability to exercise his power in that way. It does not directly follow that there is some power that God lacks. And if the act-description itself is incoherent, such as 'create a married bachelor,' it does not follow that God lacks anything at all, save perhaps the opportunity to exercise his perfect power in response to the act-description with which he is presented, since an incoherent act-description does not present even a possible candidate for action. And, remembering Kenny's stricture on what can count as a power, we can see that from the fact that God cannot act in such a way as to satisfy all the requirements of an incoherent act-description A, we cannot infer under any conditions that there is a power-to-A which God thus lacks. The relevance of all this should now be explained.

The critic is asking whether God can create a certain kind of stone—a stone which is such that he, a being who by supposition is omnipotent, cannot lift it, or cause it to rise. What is the relevant act-description here? It seems to be 'creating a stone that even a being with every logically possible power can't lift.' But what would such a stone be like? What, for example, would it weigh? If God is omnipotent, then, presumably, he can create stones of any possible weight. But if he is omnipotent, then, presumably as well, for any possible weight n, he can lift stones of weight n. Realizing this has led some philosophers to one of the simplest solutions which has been offered to the stone paradox. They have just claimed that 'creating a stone which even an omnipotent being can't lift,' and all its analytical equivalents, is just an incoherent act-description. And since the phrase 'the power to create a stone which even an omnipotent being can't lift' does not designate a logically possible power, it does not follow from the fact that God cannot create such a stone that God lacks any power required for omnipotence, or that he lacks in any other respect. This solution maintains that the proper answer to our original question is no, but that does not cause any problems for the ascription of omnipotence to God.

Other philosophers remain unconvinced that we have here an incoherent act-description. They suggest that even if it is impossible to specify the weight or size of a stone that would render it unliftable by an omnipotent being, there still might be a possible form or source of immobility which can't be overcome even by God. One suggestion is that if God is supposed to be truly omnipotent, why couldn't he create a stone which was endowed with the property of being essentially unliftable, though not because of its weight, or size, or any such distinct feature. Why couldn't there just be a stone which directly, not because of or through other properties, has the property of being impossible to lift or move? And if such a stone is possible, then surely the creation of such a stone is possible as well. So if God cannot create it, then he lacks a power it is possible to have.

It may be difficult to imagine how something could be a physical object and have the property of being necessarily immobile or unliftable. What would account for such a property? How would it work? By means of what possible laws could it operate? But even if such a property is in the end inconceivable, such philosophers could suggest, couldn't God just create an ordinary stone and promise never to move it, thereby rendering it true that he subsequently cannot lift it? And, implausible as such a scenario might be, if it is possible, then the answer to our question is not no after all but rather yes: God can create a stone he cannot lift.

But any action from which God is debarred by having made a promise is not, in virtue of its inaccessibility to him, thereby indicative of a lack of *power*. This would clearly be a case in which God lacks not a certain *ability* but a *moral capability* of doing the evil of breaking his promise. So there is a potential threat to omnipotence only from the less likely, or more perplexing, possibility of a stone he brought into existence with the essential property of unliftability, or immobility.

Suppose for a moment that God could create and did create such a stone S. Should we then say that God lacks the power to lift S? Is there a discrete power properly individuated as "the power to lift S"? Well, in Kenny's sense, there is no such possible power, for if S is essentially unliftable, there can be no single exercise of a "power to lift S." Thus, lacking a power to lift S is not lacking a possible power, a power possible to have, and so no such lack would detract from God's being omnipotent.

I shall not argue for just one of these two possible solutions to the paradox of the stone. Either will suffice. If we choose to say that God *cannot* create a stone he can't lift, we can block the inference to his lacking omnipotence and explain the apparent divine inability by characterizing the act-description here as incoherent. If we choose to say that he *can* create such a stone which, once created, he cannot lift, we can block the inference to his lacking omnipotence by explaining that the subsequent inability to lift cannot be thought of as reflecting the lack of any power it is possible to have. But by either strategy the claim of omnipotence for God is defended.

What can seem at first to be such a trivial puzzle, a silly little brain-teaser, can thus force us to clarify for ourselves much about the logic of act-descriptions, powers and ascriptions of perfection to God. It even helps us to see that the Anselmian conception of God can often be defended without our having to take definitive stands on difficult issues. The stone paradox shows that sometimes, regardless of what reasonable theistic stand we take, there is a plausible defense available for the claim that God is perfect in some respect, in this case with respect to his power.

Many critics of theism in the recent past have prematurely announced the demise of rational belief in God precisely because they have not understood the conceptual dynamics of the Christian idea of God. At the core of our idea of God is the conception of a greatest possible creator. This core conception is highly abstract and in itself very difficult to attack directly. It is the focus of the Christian's theistic convictions, as I understand them. This is the inner ring of secure conceptual commitment. But then there are the various possible developments, or elaborations, of that core conception by means of value intuitions and metaphysical argument. These more specific elaborations of the divine attributes which comprise God's perfection constitute a second level of conceptual commitment, a more fluid level of conviction. A theist very sure about his core concept of God can be much more tentative, open-minded and unsure about various possible detailed explications of the attributes of deity. But it is at this level of greater specificity that critical arguments usually arise. The critic believes he has created a problem for some attempted specification of a divine attribute, such as omnipotence, and consequently announces that the concept of God is flawed or that the attribute of omnipotence is incoherent.

The arguments of critics can be very helpful to theists, because if they are good they can steer us away from faulty specifications of the nature of divine perfection; whereas, if they are themselves flawed, our effort required to see their flaws can help us to understand better the nature of the truth at which we have arrived. The paradox of the stone allows us to see how the understanding of omnipotence in terms of powers possessed works, and the existence of two possible ways of solving it allows us to see the conceptual room available to the theist, who need not make detailed commitments on all relevant matters in order to defend his view and come to understand it better.

In just the last few years another problem relating to omnipotence has emerged. A number of philosophers have suggested that necessary goodness is incompatible with omnipotence. The argument goes like this: If God is supposed to be omnipotent, he is supposed to have every power it is logically possible to possess. Now, surely, it is logically possible to possess the power to sin. This is a power all too common among human beings. So it is a power which should be ascribed to an omnipotent being, in accordance with the definition or explication of omnipotence we are using. But one cannot have the power to perform a certain type of action A unless it is possible for one to perform actions of this type. Possibility is required for power. But we have just argued in the previous chapter that it is proper for the perfect being theologian to think of God as necessarily good, as being such that it is impossible for him to sin. On the perspective of perfect being theology, then, God must lack the power to sin. And so, on this way of thinking, he cannot be ascribed omnipotence after all.

There are two possible ways of responding to this objection. First, we could acknowledge that there is a special, discrete power to sin, a power humans have and God lacks. Along these lines, we would then have to revise our conception of the magnitude of divine power. We might still want to call God 'omnipotent,' but we would then have to qualify Kenny's account of what this means and offer something like the more restrictive gloss:

(P) God has every power it is logically possible for a being perfect in every other respect to possess.

This strategy for reconciling ascriptions of perfect goodness and omnipotence to God might be judged effective as long as three important theistic beliefs about God's power were respected by any such restriction:

(1) There can be no independent, externally determined constraints on God's power.

God is sovereign in the world. He is not hemmed in by any other competitive power. If moral principles are then thought of as constraints on God's power, morality cannot be thought of as independent of, or external to, God. How morality can be thought to be ultimately dependent on God will be indicated in the context of chapter eight, our consideration of divine creation.

(2) The internally determined structure and scope of God's possibilities of action (the limits on divine action set by God's own nature and decisions) are not, and cannot be, such that he lacks any power which otherwise would be ingredient in perfection.

Neither God's nature, in its other facets, nor his decisions can have a negative impact on the perfection of the power available to him. Perfection is not self-destructive or self-undermining. Finally,

(3) God is the sole source of all the power there is or could be.

This assurance, along with a strong conception of divine goodness and wisdom, disallows the implication following from the restricted account of divine power that there could even possibly be a being with all the power God does have *plus* a power to sin, a being independent of God who could possibly, through the having of this greater total array of power, ultimately thwart God's purposes and plans. With all this in mind, a restricted account of God's power could be a usable solution to the problem raised by the apparent existence of a power to sin.

But the best solution to this problem, I think, will involve denying that there is a discrete causal power to sin. If, following the developments of the last chapter, we do hold that God is necessarily good, we do believe that it is impossible that God sin. This can be stated by saying that God cannot sin. But it may be sheer carelessness to think that this is the same as saying, or that it even implies, that God lacks some power, namely, what has been, so far, loosely referred to as "the power to sin."

How do we identify discrete powers? The idea of a power is a very fundamental notion. We typically identify powers with a certain standard locution, employing the infinitives of verbs along with verb phrases. We speak, for example, of "the power to lift one hundred pounds," "the power to communicate through an earthly language," "the power to create a stone." Now there are, no doubt, many sorts of powers of which we have no conception and for which we have no ready-made power locutions of this type. But in another respect, our language is much richer than the underlying metaphysical realities having to do with power. For consider the two phrases (power locutions):

(A) the power to lift a blue two-ounce pencil
(B) the power to lift a yellow two-ounce pencil.

I have whatever power is designated by (A). I have whatever power is designated by (B). The power locutions (A) and (B) are two distinct locutions. It doesn't follow that they express two different powers, or that by being able to lift blue and yellow pencils I should be credited with two different powers. There is, presumably, only one basic power referred to differently by these two different power phrases.

So, distinct power locutions are no guarantee of correspondingly distinct powers. Nor is the mere existence of a power locution of the appropriate form any guarantee that there is a discrete power referred to by the phrase. Consider as an extreme instance: 'the power to see to it that there never were any powers at all.' There cannot be a discrete power referred to by this phrase. And whatever power is referred to by (A) and (B) has absolutely nothing intrinsically to do with anything regarding color. The surface grammar of power locutions can be misleading in numerous ways.

Following an example once presented by St. Anselm, we can see that to say of a certain man that "he cannot lose in battle" is not to attribute to him any lack of power. It attributes any real lack only to his enemies.[5] Likewise, to say of God that he cannot sin, should not be taken to imply on God's part any lack of power. It only indicates a necessarily firm directedness in the way in which God will *use* his unlimited power.

I would like to suggest that there is no discrete power referred to by the phrase 'the power to sin.' There are many powers necessary for sinning in various ways, but there is no single, distinct power to sin exercised in addition to all other powers exercised on any and every occasion of the intentional doing of evil. Suppose Jones wrongfully hits Smith in the face, intending to cause him pain. Jones must have and exercise the power to make a fist, the power to swing and aim his fist, and so forth, in order to commit the deed. Does he need an additional causal power once he has all those physical powers, a distinct power to sin? I do not think so. Drawing upon the chart presented earlier in this chapter, we could say that Jones is capable of using his power in a way a more saintly person would not, and in a way a perfect person could not. The difference is not in the powers possessed, but in the moral capacity for employing those powers.

To account for why it is that a certain person cannot perform a certain kind of act we need not, and should not, always suppose that a lack of power is what is involved. In the present case, to account for why God cannot do evil we need not, and should not, attribute this divine guarantee to inability or lack of power. It is due, rather, entirely to God's perfection of character. There is no power to sin which God lacks. So there is here no exception to his being thought of as altogether omnipotent after all.

But the following problem could be raised. Even if it is granted that there is no incoherence about the ascription of omnipotence to God, and even if there is no glaring counterexample to the claim that God has every power it is logically possible to possess, how can the positive ascription of omnipotence ever be justified? To defend omnipotence against objections is not yet to provide any positive ground for thinking of God as omnipotent. And it can be thought that the provision of a positive ground would be impossible.

How do we justify power ascriptions? Typically, on the basis of observation. We see a person perform an action or range of actions and ascribe to him whatever kind or degree of power would be necessary for the performance we have witnessed. But under what conditions could any finite number of observations of divine conduct warrant or justify the ascription of omnipotence to God? Suppose God somehow were observed performing extraordinary miracles, in whatever mode of observation is appropriate. Would any number of such dramatic actions legitimate the claim that God has every power it is logically possible to possess? Suppose we know God to have created the entire existent universe. Would even *that* piece of astounding information call for the postulation of omnipotence, and nothing less? It is hard to see how any finite observations and data could ever demand, or even justify, so extreme an ascription of power as that ingredient in the attribution of omnipotence. And if this is so, one recent writer has suggested, not only could *we* never know or justifiably believe that God is omnipotent, he himself could not know or justifiably believe it. For, no matter how many tough tasks he proposed to himself and accomplished without the least effort, the literal ascription, or self-ascription, of omnipotence would go beyond the theoretical demands of explaining the observations made.[6] Omnipotence is that extreme a notion.

The answer to this challenge is actually simple. First, God does not come to know himself inferentially, from making observations about his own conduct and extrapolating from those observations to their best theoretical explanations. God knows himself directly, as St. Thomas Aquinas taught us.[7] Second, we do not have to rely upon observation and inference for all our ascriptions of properties to God. We hold that God is literally omnipotent because of the requirements of perfect being theology, as it encapsulates and extends the data of revelation. We derive the belief in strict omnipotence as a divine attribute not inductively from observation, but deductively from the conceptual and intuitive resources of perfect being theology. As a perfect being, God is perfect in power. We are justified in thinking of God as perfect in this respect, as in every other, unless there is well-attested revelation or credible human experience to the contrary. Observation is a constraint upon, but not the sole source of, our ideas about God.

5

God's
Knowledge

*I*t is often said that knowledge is power. And while, as careful thinkers, we must keep these two concepts distinct, we must also acknowledge some truth in this saying. Knowledge is the precondition for any intelligent, rational use of power. And knowledge is an enabler. The more knowledge a person has, the more scope he has for the exercise of his power. In the previous chapter, we have explored the idea that God is perfect in power. In this chapter, we shall examine the related claim that he is perfect in knowledge as well.

The Nature of God's Knowledge

If knowledge is an intrinsic good, then the property of being knowledgeable is a great-making property. And if the value of knowledge is additive ("the more the better"), then to have total knowledge is greater than to have incomplete knowledge. Most practitioners of perfect being theology have judged that God must be ascribed great knowledge and that, befitting his perfection, God's knowledge must be utterly complete. To be only a bit more precise, God's knowledge is thought to be as complete as it is possible for a state of knowledge to be.

One aspect of the perfection of God's knowledge is then its completeness. Another aspect is its directness. From the point of view of perfect being theology, God cannot be conceived of as having to depend for his knowledge on any independent sources, intermediaries or carriers of information. Unlike us, he does not have to rely upon sense organs or the testimony of others for truth about his world. His knowledge rather consists in his being in the most intimate contact possible with the objects of that knowledge. In brief, God's knowledge is as direct as it is possible for a state of knowledge to be.

The conception of God's knowledge as both complete and direct can thus be motivated by thinking along the lines of perfect being theology. It can also arise from reflecting on what is involved in his being absolute creator of all. In the Christian tradition, creation is thought of as a thoroughly intelligent and rational activity. God is not a blind fountain of being, but is rather a wise and provident designer of what there is. Recall that creation theology thinks of God as responsible for the being of everything that exists distinct from himself, and as himself being such that nothing else could possibly exist without having him as its creator. It is hard to imagine how his creative responsibility could in this way be complete and rational without his knowledge being complete. And how could such a creator God be thought to depend on any intermediary for his knowledge? For he would have to be conceived of equally as the creator of both the intermediary and the ultimate object of knowledge. But then, given the thoroughgoing intelligence and rationality of creation, he *as creator* would have to be every bit as well acquainted with the properties of the object as of the intermediary. And of course this renders the supposition of an intermediary, and the very idea of its function, utterly otiose. God cannot be thought to depend on an intermediary—a person, faculty, sense organ or signal—for his knowledge of a distinct object when in order to be the creator of both the intermediary and the object, he would have to know them equally well from the start.

The idea of God as a perfect knower which we can derive from both perfect being theology and creation theology is not just a result of philosophical speculation. It is an idea reflected in a great number of biblical passages. In the book of Job, for example, it is said of God that "he looks to the ends of the earth and sees everything under the heavens" (Job 28:24). In the New Testament, the book of Hebrews adds that "before him no creature is hidden, but all are open and laid bare to the eyes of him with whom we have to do" (Heb 4:13). And there is no hint here of cognitive indirectness. Nothing is interposed between God and his creatures. As many biblical passages seem to make clear, God is as intimately acquainted with us his creatures as it is possible to be.[1]

Anselmian thinking, creation theology and the Bible are all mutually reinforcing on these basic ideas concerning God's knowledge. They can act as mutual constraints as well. On a simple-minded reading of some biblical passages, for example, it can appear as though God's knowledge is not after all complete. We have gotten no farther than Genesis 3:9 when we see that God asked Adam the question "Where are you?" Did he not know? And why does Jeremiah represent God as "searching the human heart"? Does he not know what is in the heart until he searches it? Perfect being theology and creation theology can assure us that this is not the way to read such passages. When God asks a question, he seeks to teach, not to be taught. We are not to infer that his knowledge is incomplete, requiring augmentation.

Likewise, biblical passages and creation theology can serve as a corrective to misapplications of perfection thinking. There is one ancient view according to which it would seem beneath the dignity of a perfect being to even bother to attend to certain details in the world. On this conception, it would be inappropriate for a being of God's exalted status to acquaint himself intimately with dirt, hair, mud and filth, to cite only a few standard examples. One application of the method of perfect being theology specifies only that God is not to be ascribed any limitations *which imply imperfection*. On this interpretation, it could be argued, as it seems to have been believed by some of the ancients, that certain bits or even kinds of knowledge are such that their lack does not imply imperfection, and thus that a perfect being is not required to have them. Of course, it is an extra step to think that such a being is required not to have them, but both the Bible and the requirements of creation theology block even the first step of this sort of theological squeamishness. We are told in the Gospels that God is concerned with the grass of the field, the birds of the air, and with every hair on our heads (Mt 6:25-32; 10:30; Lk 12). The God of the Bible is not a being with superior airs who will not or cannot condescend to make contact with the least of the items in his creation. He is not the fastidious deity of Plato's *Timaeus*, who must have lesser gods interposed between himself and the squalor of this world as buffers to guard his eminence from any taint of cognitive pollution. This is as far from the biblical idea as can be imagined. Nor will such cognitive selectivity be allowed by creation theology, which requires an absolutely universal scope to God's knowledge of what exists in this world. Any attempt to apply the methods of perfect being theology to compromise the completeness of God's knowledge in this way will thus be resisted and blocked by a consultation of the biblical documents and the demands of creation thought.

God's Knowledge and the Future: The Problem

The completeness of God's knowledge is often referred to as his *omniscience*. By claiming that God is omniscient, theists typically mean to say that

(1) God has all propositional knowledge

and

(2) God has perfect acquaintance with all things.

Propositional knowledge is, simply put, knowledge that can be expressed by indicative sentences or "that-clauses": God knows that football and philosophy are two active enterprises at Notre Dame; God knows that the earth is the third planet from the sun; God knows that 2 + 2 = 4; God knows that equality is a transitive relation; and so forth. Following a number of their medieval predecessors (who wrote in Latin), philosophers often refer to this as knowledge *de dicto*. In ordinary language we sometimes distinguish between having knowledge *about* an object or person and more directly knowing that thing or person. I may have a great deal of knowledge about guitarist Eric Clapton without its being true that I know him. I may know about Paris from reading many descriptions and histories of that city. But ordinarily, I can't be said to know Paris unless I have been there to establish intimate firsthand acquaintance with its many delights. The firsthand intimacy of knowledge by acquaintance is often referred to by philosophers as knowledge *de re*.[2] The extent of God's omniscience includes absolute completeness in both knowledge *de dicto* and knowledge *de re*.[3]

God is also thought to be *infallible* as a knower. He cannot go wrong or possibly hold any false beliefs. Not only is God omniscient, he is *necessarily omniscient*—it is impossible that his omniscience collapse, fail, or even waver. He is, as philosophers nowadays often say, omniscient in *every possible world*. That is to say, he is actually omniscient, and there is no possible, complete and coherent story about any way things could have gone (no "possible world") in which God lacks this degree of cognitive excellence.

In order to appreciate fully the status of divine knowledge, we need to make some further clarifications. The proposition that *God is omniscient* is a necessarily true proposition. There are no circumstances possible under which it is false. But the precise sense in which this is so needs to be clarified. For the proposition that *bachelors are unmarried men* is also a necessary truth, following, as it does, from the concept of bachelorhood. Yet we would never say of an individual bachelor, Ted, Fred or Ned, that *he* is necessarily unmarried. However confirmed his bachelorhood may be, however apparently hopeless his nuptial prospects might be, it is always at least *possible* for him to marry. Even concerning someone who lives and dies a bachelor, it can be said that it was at least logically or metaphysically *possible* for him to have wed. Being unmarried is a logically necessary condition of bachelorhood, but being a bachelor is not a necessary life condition of anyone who happens to be single.

The case of God's omniscience contrasts with this in an interesting way. Consider the English sentence:

(B) Bachelors are unmarried men.

This sentence expresses a proposition (roughly, the content it conveys). It expresses a truth. It expresses a necessity. But it expresses a necessity only in the sense of conveying a necessary truth with respect to the conditions of bachelorhood. The concept of bachelorhood is such that it yields (B) as a necessary truth. That is to say, (B) expresses a necessity *de dicto*. It does not express a necessity *de re*, concerning some particular individual, some particular bachelor. It does not say of any particular bachelors that *they* are necessarily unmarried men.

Now consider the English sentence:

(G) God is omniscient.

This sentence expresses a proposition. It expresses a truth, and it expresses a necessity. In much the same way that (B) serves as a partial explication of bachelorhood, (G) can be seen as a partial explication of deity. On this reading, (G) presents a necessary condition for holding the exalted position, or having the maximal status, of *being God*. It expresses a necessity *de dicto*. But most theists influenced by the method of perfect being theology insist that it expresses a necessity *de re* as well. Not only is omniscience necessary for divinity, divinity is a necessary or essential property of any individual who has it. Unlike the property of being a bachelor, which is a contingent or accidental property, the property of being God is best thought of as a necessary or essential property. An individual who is God does not just happen to have that status. It is not a property he could have done without. Things at the top are more stable than this. In particular, omniscience is as firmly rooted in God, or God is as firmly rooted in omniscience, as it is possible to be. Omniscience is thus not only a necessary condition of deity, it is a necessary or essential property for any individual who is God. No literally divine person is even possibly vulnerable to ignorance.

This distinction in levels of necessity, so to speak, is customarily captured by different forms of expression such as:

(G1) Necessarily, God is omniscient,
which standardly expresses the necessity *de dicto*, and

(G2) God is necessarily omniscient,

which standardly expresses the necessity *de re*. In fact, the most exalted form of Anselmian theology will insist that (G2) expresses a necessity *de dicto* as well: Not only is omniscience a requirement for deity, necessary or essential omniscience is as well. A being who was even possibly vulnerable to ignorance would not be a greatest possible being. So perfection requires essential omniscience.

This is a very strong picture of the state of God's knowledge. In fact, many people have thought that it is far too strong. The problem is that if God's knowledge is absolutely complete and he cannot possibly hold a false belief about anything, an argument can be constructed which seems to show that there cannot be any genuine freedom, any authentically free will, in the world at all. The problem posed by this argument is widely known as the *problem of foreknowledge and free will*.

Initially, at least, it seems that in order for God's knowledge to be absolutely complete, he must know everything about the past, everything about the present, and everything about the future as well. But if he now knows, and always has known, how each and every one of us will act, in every detail, on every occasion in the future, how can we possibly be thought to be free in our actions, selecting among alternatives equally available to us? If God already knows exactly how we *shall* act, what else can we possibly do? We must act in that way. We cannot diverge from the path that he sees we shall take. We cannot prove God wrong. He is necessarily omniscient. Divine foreknowledge thus seems to preclude genuine alternatives, and thus genuine freedom in the world.

Notice that nothing has been said here about complete divine *predestination*, which is an exercise of God's *power* to determine the future in each and every detail. This argument has arisen solely from a consideration of the completeness of God's *knowledge*. In order to appreciate the distinctiveness of the problem posed by foreknowledge, let us first linger a bit over the distinct idea of total predestination.

Some theists endorse the idea that God has eternally predestined, or predetermined, the course of history in every detail. God is, remember, to be thought of as the omnipotent creator of all things. It is typically taken to be a corollary of this that God is sovereign over all things. He is, in the most ultimate way possible, in control of all things, however unlikely this may sometimes appear. So far, most theists are in agreement. Where total predestinarians diverge from other theists is in their interpretation of what such sovereign control requires. It is their contention that God could not be in complete control of the course of history unless he himself authored the story in all its details. Thus, they conclude, God predestines, or foreordains, or predetermines all things. But then, consider the following simple argument:

(1) God's power is irresistible.

Thus,

(2) For any event x, if God determines x, then no one is in a position to prevent x.

(3) For any event x, if no one is in a position to prevent x, then no one is free with respect to x.

(4) For every event x, God determines x.

Therefore,

(5) No one distinct from God is free with respect to any event.

And so,

(6) Human free will is a complete illusion.

In this argument, premise (1) follows from our understanding of the perfection of God's power. Line (2) is an immediate consequence of (1). Line (3) results from our ordinary conception of what it is to be free. Line (4) presents the thesis of total predestination. And finally, lines (5) and (6) draw the sad conclusions from these previous steps.

In so far as most theists believe that we are free, and thus morally responsible, for at least a great many of our actions, they reject (5) and (6), and so must reject one of the steps leading up to (5) and (6). The weak link in the argument is typically judged to be line (4), the thesis of total predestination, and so that view is rejected, in order to preserve the more deeply entrenched belief in human freedom. And, fortunately for those of us convinced of the reality of human freedom, whatever its limitations, it is possible to understand God's sovereignty as involving less than the predetermination of every detail of cosmic history. A teacher can be in control of a classroom without herself causing every move the students make. In order to endorse God's omnipotence, recognize his creation of all, and acknowledge his ultimate control of things, it is not necessary to embrace the doctrine of total predestination.

The challenge of foreknowledge has seemed to many people a little less easy to shake. It is a good deal more natural to suppose that the completeness of God's knowledge requires a full awareness of what the future holds than it is to suppose that the completeness of his control of creation requires that he causally predetermines everything that ever happens in the world. And the biblical documents seem to contain a great many instances of prophecy or prediction which appear to be based on a divine foreknowledge of the future.[4] So the idea that God is a perfect knower of the future must be taken very seriously indeed.

But, as we have noted, this creates a problem. To appreciate the force of that problem, we should lay out a single straightforward argument, as we did for the idea of total predestination. Stating such an argument will help us to see the interrelation of ideas which generate the problem. To make everything as clear as possible, we'll start from a claim about God's *beliefs*, rather than stating the argument in terms of his knowledge. Whenever someone knows something, we can distinguish the object of knowledge, or the fact that is known, on the one hand, from the knower's mental state of belief, or awareness, by means of which he is connected with what is known, on the other hand. For God to have complete foreknowledge of the future is for him to have comprehensive belief states, or states of awareness, concerning the future, which constitute knowledge. With this in mind, and picking up on the claims about God's necessary omniscience, we have:

(1) God's beliefs are infallible.

Thus,

(2) For any event *x*, if God believes in advance that *x* will occur, then no one is in a position to prevent *x*.

(3) For any event *x*, if no one is in a position to prevent *x*, then no one is free with respect to *x*.

(4) For every event *x* that ever occurs, God believes in advance that it will occur.

Therefore,

(5) No one distinct from God is free with respect to any event.

And so,

(6) Human free will is a complete illusion.

What we have here is an argument perfectly parallel in form to the argument for the incompatibility of predestination and free will. Premise (1) expresses the conviction that God cannot possibly go wrong in his beliefs. This is an implication of his essential omniscience. Line (2) of the argument draws quickly the further implication that no one is free to act in such a way as to falsify one of God's beliefs. Step (3) unpacks part of our standard conception of what it is to be free with respect to something. Line (4) presents the thesis of complete divine foreknowledge. And lines (5) and (6) draw the inferences from what has preceded which seem so troubling.

Reactions to the Problem

Thoughtful religious believers have reacted in many different ways to arguments like the one just presented. Some have felt compelled by this sort of reasoning to deny that we ever do have genuine freedom in what we do. And once freedom is given up, there is no longer any good reason to reject the total predestination interpretation of divine sovereignty. But few theists are willing to embrace so extreme a conclusion as the belief that we are never really free, never really faced with genuine options or alternatives of action, any one of which we are equally in a position to take. Most of us have such a deep and firm conviction that we are at least sometimes free in what we do, in precisely this sense, that we shall seek in any way possible to resist a philosophical argument which purports to show the contrary. Moreover, the Bible itself and other central theological doctrines seem to presuppose that we are free, and thus morally responsible for our sins as well as for whether or not we seek the proper relation with our creator. Thus, the outright denial of freedom is not a popular response to this argument and arguments of its type.

The harsh conclusions expressed by lines (5) and (6) of the argument can be avoided if we redefine "free will" in such a way that freedom doesn't require genuine options or alternatives for action. The view of freedom as compatible with a lack of options is, naturally enough, known as *compatibilism*. If compatibilism concerning free action is true, it can be argued that line (3) of the argument is false. The compatibilist suggestion is, roughly, that in order to be free with respect to an action, or with respect to the initiation of a train of events, I need not be in a position to refrain from performing the act or to prevent the sequence of events. I am free so long as my activity is in keeping with my intentions or desires in the matter, even if there are no genuine alternatives open to me. Thus, for the compatibilist, whether I have the power, or ability, or opportunity to deviate from the path God already believes I shall take is just irrelevant to the question of whether I am free in what I do. And if this is right, premise (3) of the argument we are examining is just false, and thus we are free to reject its conclusions.

Not many theists, however, have managed to content themselves with a compatibilist view of freedom. Most insist that in order to determine whether an action is free, we need to ask not only whether it occurs in harmony with the desires, choices and intentions of its agent, but also whether those affective and volitional states—those desires, choices and intentions—are themselves such that the agent could have refrained from, or prevented himself from, having them. In accordance with this, most theists hold that the ideal paradigm of free action does involve having real alternatives available. Of course, in the Christian world-view, God himself is viewed as the paradigmatically free agent. And he is held to be supremely free in precisely this sense. He is never without real alternatives. So, on a Christian scheme of things, freedom is most naturally viewed as involving alternatives.

The belief that genuine freedom, on any level, is *not* compatible with an utter lack of any real options is known, naturally enough, as *incompatibilism*. (This is the conception of freedom ingredient in the philosophical view known as *libertarianism*, the traditional view that we often are at liberty to originate our own lines of conduct.) An incompatibilist on the issue of how we should understand genuine freedom will insist on acknowledging the truth of premise (3) of our argument. So anyone who endorses this view of freedom, and is committed to the libertarian thesis that we are free, will have to find another point at which to resist this argument for the conclusion that we are never really free.

One possible strategy consists in the attempt to block the inference from premise (1),

God's beliefs are infallible,

to line (2),

For any event *x*, if God believes in advance that *x* will occur, then no one is in a position to prevent *x*.

In recent discussions of the problem of foreknowledge and free will, at least two versions of this strategy have been attempted. Some philosophers, who endorse a view known as *Ockhamism* (a view influenced by the great medieval thinker William of Ockham), have argued basically as follows: Suppose God has always believed that in exactly five minutes my right index finger will lightly scratch the tip of my nose. God is necessarily omniscient and so, as a believer, he is absolutely infallible. He cannot be wrong. Does it follow that no one is in a position to prevent it from being the case that, nearly five minutes hence, my finger will scratch my nose? Does it follow, in particular, that I am not free with respect to scratching? No, the Ockhamists insist, all that follows is that I *shall* scratch, not that I *must*, or that I lack the power to refrain from scratching. I can prevent the event in question. I can refrain from scratching. This option is open to me. I shall not take it, as a matter of fact, but the alternative is there. And, the Ockhamists add, if I did refrain from scratching, I would not prove God wrong. For if I were to exercise this option and leave the tip of my nose alone, God would have held a belief different from the one he in fact holds—he always would have believed that I would, at the appointed time, have done something else with my right index finger rather than scratching my nose. So the Ockhamists hold that for this event *x*, I am in a position to prevent *x*, but as a matter of fact will freely perform *x* instead. Generalizing, step (2) cannot legitimately be inferred from step (1) in our argument. But without this, the argument collapses and the problem with freedom is avoided.

The difficulty with the Ockhamist strategy is that, presumably, God has already held one particular determinate belief about what I shall do at the time in question. We have been supposing that he has always believed that I shall scratch. How then can I be said to have the option not to do this at the appointed time? I have a real option only if, in the circumstances, I can exercise it. But, by supposition, my circumstances include my already having been seen, or believed, to do one thing by God, a being who cannot possibly be wrong. We cannot change what already has been. It is not plausible to think that I can act in such a way as to alter what God's belief has already been. Thus it seems that, given all my circumstances (including everything that is already true), I cannot refrain from scratching and so, despite what the Ockhamist says, I shall not be free with respect to that action. And, of course, given the completeness of God's knowledge, this consideration generalizes to all human actions at all times. If the Ockhamist insists that I can now act in such a way as to *change*, or otherwise determine what God's beliefs in the remote past already were concerning what I shall do, then he swims upstream against some pretty strong intuitions most people have about the impossibility of changing or affecting the past in any substantive way whatsoever.

There is one other attempt to solve the problem of foreknowledge and free will which seeks to block the inference of step (2) from step (1) in the argument we are considering. It draws upon the work of another medieval thinker, Luis de Molina, and goes by the name of *Molinism*. The Molinist view is based on a distinctive conception of the makeup of God's knowledge. The range of divine knowledge is thought of as divided into three types: *natural knowledge*—knowledge God has prior to (conceptually prior to) any act of creation, concerning what all the possibilities of creation are; *free knowledge*—knowledge of everything that will actually happen in the world *given* God's free choice of which possibilities of creation to actualize; and *middle knowledge*—comprehensive knowledge of what contingently, as a matter of fact, *would* result from any creative decision he might make. In this threefold categorization, it is the category of middle knowledge which is most important. Middle knowledge is supposed to encompass an infinite array of propositions sometimes referred to by philosophers as subjunctive conditionals of freedom or, in a slightly less precise but more widely used terminology, *counterfactuals of freedom*. Simply put, a counterfactual of freedom is a proposition specifying how a free being would freely act if placed in a certain total set of circumstances. It is a proposition of the form: If placed in total circumstances C, person P would freely perform action A. The Molinist supposes that for every created person who could possibly exist, every total array of circumstances he could possibly exist in, and every action he could possibly perform, there is a truth of this form. For example, I suppose that there are many total sets of circumstances in which, if I were offered one hundred dollars to refrain from eating lunch just once this week and go jogging for an hour instead, I would freely skip that meal with great pleasure. I would have the alternative of sticking to my ordinary schedule and not missing a meal. And it would be a genuine alternative. It's just true that I would not take that alternative. I would freely take the money and run. Now, the main way in which it seems that the typical Molinist proposes to reconcile foreknowledge and human freedom is by explaining *how* God foreknows the future free actions of his creatures in every detail. The story is basically very simple. Knowing how every individual he could possibly create would freely act in every complete set of circumstances he could possibly be placed in, God, by deciding who to create and what circumstances to create them in, completely provides himself with the knowledge of everything that will ever happen.

On the Molinist view, line (2) of our argument does not follow from line (1) and is not true because, to use our previous example, God's past belief that I shall scratch my nose is based on his knowing that if I were created and put in certain circumstances (involving, say, a sufficiently itchy nose) then I would *freely* scratch the tip of my nose with my right index finger, along with his deciding to create me in such a way that I would be in those circumstances at the right time. So, when the time comes, it cannot be said, as line (2) of our argument says, that "no one is in a position to prevent x." If I am truly free with respect to scratching, *I* am in a position to prevent its happening, by simply refraining from that action. God knows that I shall freely pass up that option, but it is an option I have. The counterfactual of freedom which provided for God's belief and thus his foreknowledge was precisely that—a counterfactual, or subjunctive conditional, *of freedom.* Molinism may provide the greatest hope for reconciling divine foreknowledge and human freedom.[5] Unlike Ockhamism, it offers an interesting account of how God is able to know the future. And it carries no hint of an implication that, in order to be free, I must be able to act in such a way as to change or determine what God's beliefs about me have already been. It also goes a long way toward explicating a strong traditional view of God's providential governance of the world. And it puts questions about predestination in a new light. But it is a position which depends on many complex and controversial assumptions. How, for example, can the infinitely many counterfactuals of freedom which are supposed to be true attain that status prior to the creation of any people at all? What makes them true? There are serious questions which can be raised about any answer to this question that is attempted. The resources of Molinism may provide for the most exalted conception of God's knowledge and providential care imaginable, but their integrity, plausibility and efficacy have not yet been established. And to some critics, the same problem plaguing Ockhamism will just seem to rear its ugly head once more: How can there possibly be truths and infallible divine beliefs about what I shall freely do far in advance of any deliberation and decision making on my part? If there are truths and infallible divine beliefs about what I shall do, it is hard to see how they can really be beliefs and truths about what I shall do *freely*. Unless I can refrain from scratching my nose, really refrain, regardless of my circumstances, I do not scratch freely. I do not have genuine options, and line (2) of our argument is after all, despite all that Molinists say to the contrary, true. This is a criticism it is not altogether easy to dismiss.

But there are at least two other strategies for responding to our argument which are well worth mentioning, however briefly. They both reject, in different ways, premise (4) of the argument, the claim that:

For every event *x* that ever occurs, God believes in advance that it will occur.

And they both attempt to do this in a way which does not detract from our being able to endorse the completeness of God's knowledge. In other respects, they are as different as can be imagined.

Many great philosophers and theologians of the past, including Augustine, Boethius, Anselm and Aquinas, have believed that God exists outside the boundaries of time. He is not a temporal or time-bound being at all. Let us refer to this theological view as *atemporal eternalism*. According to atemporal eternalism, God does not believe anything *in advance* of the occurrence of anything, because to hold a belief, or to do anything, *prior to* or *in advance of* anything else is to be a temporal being subject to time. So when the time arrives for me, or for you, to make a decision or to choose one avenue of action over another, God has not *already* held a belief concerning exactly what will be done, and so it seems that there is nothing in our temporal circumstances to prevent our having a real array of options equally available to us. Another way of putting this is to say that God's eternal knowledge of our actions is more like simultaneous knowledge than it is like advance knowledge. And just as your simultaneous knowledge that I am now scratching my nose does not detract in the least from the freedom of the act, so likewise, the atemporal eternalist assures us, God's eternal knowledge of my scratching does not inhibit at all its freedom.

The doctrine of atemporal divine eternity is itself a very difficult notion which will be explored more fully in the next chapter. Here it is important to point out only that it is difficult to see how its claim about God and time can alone reconcile the completeness of divine knowledge concerning our future with the reality of human freedom. Of course, if God is outside time, then premise (4) as it is stated is false, and so the precise argument we have been examining is blocked. But then a comparable argument for the same conclusions could be built around a slightly emended fourth premise:

(4') For every event x that ever occurs, God eternally believes that it will occur,

along with a correspondingly altered second line,

(2') For any event x, if God believes eternally that x occurs, then no one is in a position to prevent x.

And if (2') is true, the eternalist move alone will not suffice to reconcile the completeness of God's knowledge with our being genuinely free.

In order to evaluate the truth of (2'), we need to reflect for a moment on the following consideration. On the atemporal eternalist picture, God is related equally to all moments of time, in terms of his knowledge and power. But if that is so then, presumably, he could have revealed to someone ten years ago his eternal knowledge that at a certain point in our future I shall scratch my nose. So suppose he has done this. Note that to be consistent with the atemporal eternalist view, we cannot say that ten years ago God made this revelation. He is not in time and does not act *at* times. But we can suppose that ten years ago someone received a revelation which God eternally willed to be received at that time (again, there will be more on this in the next chapter), a revelation containing one piece of God's eternal cluster of beliefs, the information that at a certain time t, I shall scratch the tip of my nose in a certain way. When t arrives, will I be in a position to refrain from scratching and prove this revelation false? Surely not, for God is an infallible believer (the first premise of our argument) and God cannot lie (because of his necessary goodness). So it seems that even if God were atemporally eternal, outside of time, were such a revelation to be granted, I would be just as hemmed in as I would be if God had temporal foreknowledge of my actions.

What is important to note here is that whether God happens to reveal his eternal beliefs about our temporal actions or whether he keeps them to himself should not alone make any difference to whether we are free or not. It is not at all clear that, or how it could be the case that, it would be the act or fact of revelation itself that would act as a constraint.[6] For, as critics of the eternalist strategy here have argued, whether God reveals it or not, on our assumptions it could have been truly said or believed by anyone ten years ago that God eternally knows that I shall scratch. And thus *it was true* ten years ago that God eternally sees this scratching at t. But this is enough to create the problem, to entail that at no time prior to t was anyone in a position to act in such a way that no scratching occurs at t. And this just means that we still have a problem concerning the completeness of God's knowledge, as it encompasses what is future to *us*, and our being free.

In fairness to this atemporal eternalist view, however, I should point out that not all philosophers are persuaded that, for any action x and time t, if I perform x at t, then at any time before t it was then true that I shall do x at t. Likewise a philosopher can resist the inference from "God eternally believes that I do x at t" to "ten years before t it was true that God eternally believes that I do x at t." If this inference can be blocked, then perhaps some way can be devised for an eternalist to forge an argument for the compatibility of complete divine knowledge, encompassing our future and genuine free will. Perhaps this will involve the eternalist embracing the idea of middle knowledge and transposing it into an atemporal key, but to pursue this suggestion here would lead us into more complexities than our present purpose allows.

The eternalist tries to preserve the absolute completeness of God's knowledge and by locating God and that knowledge outside time to block the argument against free will. The suggestion is that God's knowledge of our future is not literally *fore*knowledge, and thus that premise (4) of the argument is strictly false. There is another response to the argument that consists in denying that there is complete divine foreknowledge of the future, and thus in rejecting premise (4). But this strategy sees God as a temporal being who is everlasting—existing at each and every moment of time—and so it is a strategy which cannot seek to protect the completeness of God's knowledge by locating it in an atemporally eternal level of reality. It is a view which has been developed in recent years in interestingly different ways by a number of philosophers, including Peter Geach, J. R. Lucas, George Schlesinger and William Hasker.[7] For the lack of any better-established name, we shall refer to it as *presentism*.

According to the Ockhamist, the Molinist, the atemporal eternalist, and the adherents of most other traditional views, the completeness of God's knowledge includes his having a comprehensive array of beliefs concerning everything in our future, in the most minute detail imaginable. The future is already, or eternally, known to God, and the passage of time is like the unrolling of a rug whose pattern has long been established. But this is not the view of presentism. According to the presentist, the future does not yet exist to be known. The forward edge of determinate reality is the present, and what comes next is no more than a realm of the possible and the probable. The passage of time is more like the weaving together of a rug afresh rather than the mere unrolling of one already there. And in a nondeterministic world, the results of this weaving cannot always be predicted. In particular, the free actions of human beings and other rational creatures cannot possibly be infallibly foreknown. Nor can they be eternally ascertained. As a perfect knower, God knows all possibilities for the developments in his creation. He knows what has occurred in every detail. And he is, in the words of Schlesinger, a perfect diagnostician of present tendencies. He knows present dispositions, proclivities, inclinations, intentions and probabilities as well as they can be known. But in a world which is not deterministic, in a world peopled by free beings, this does not give him the whole future story of creation. In the very last sentence of a recent book treating this issue, J. R. Lucas says:

If God created man in his own image, He must have created him capable of new initiatives and new insights which cannot be precisely or infallibly foreknown, but which give to the future a perpetual freshness as the inexhaustible variety of possible thoughts and actions, on the part of his children as well as himself, crystallizes into actuality.[8]

On this view, God's knowledge is as complete as it is possible for a state of knowledge to be, *given the sort of world which exists to be known.* The existence of freedom does preclude infallible foreknowledge, just as the latter prevents the former. But human freedom is no illusion. Thus, the perfect completeness of God's knowledge should not be understood to include comprehensive infallible beliefs concerning everything in the future. This is another way of rejecting premise (4) of our original argument, the premise which lays down the doctrine of complete foreknowledge.

As a response to the argument and as a view of God, presentism can be thought to have a couple of theological drawbacks. First, it offers a distinctively weaker conception of divine providence than what is provided by the more traditional view of Molinism. God does not have comprehensive access to our future, in all its details. Nor can he plan all in advance, if he leaves us truly free. Unanticipated innovations can occur in the created realm. Nothing, however, will utterly and fundamentally surprise God, on the presentist view. For he does know all possibilities. And nothing can ultimately thwart his plans, because of the perfect range of his power. So even though he cannot, on this view, foresee all future developments in his creation, we can nonetheless be assured that in the end his kingdom will prevail. It's just that, for presentism, the sort of meticulous providence allowed for by the Molinist is not a possibility. Of course, this may be judged by many theists not to be such a drawback after all. For it may make it a lot easier for us to deal with the problem of evil. On the Molinist view, God chooses all that will occur, including everything we judge to be evil. On the presentist view, it can be held that this aspect of creaturely history is just allowed, not planned, by God.

Second, it can be considered a weakness for presentism that this view has a greater difficulty accounting for the reliability of biblical prophecies, some of which seem to be about free actions and seem to capture both accurately and in advance quite specific details about what is to be (see for example Mt 11:27 and Mk 14:27-30). Are the prophecies to be viewed as no more than the best divine extrapolations possible from present tendencies, which just happened, fortunately, to come true? Or do they all involve situations which were not, after all, situations involving genuine human freedom, but rather circumstances in which God himself acted in such a way as to see to it that what was predicted came to pass? Either supposition involves difficulties. But this is not to say that those difficulties cannot be overcome. There are ways in which the presentist can seek to offer a plausible account of biblical prophecies. Some prophecies are not so specific. Others seem somewhat conditional, rather than being outright, determinate predictions. It's just that more traditional views of the completeness of God's knowledge seem to have available more natural explanations for the accuracy of prophetic prediction in the Bible.

At the present time, there is no consensus among Christian or theistic philosophers, or among theologians, concerning which is the best response to the argument from foreknowledge (or divine forebelief) to the nonexistence of free will. It may be that something like a Molinist eternalism would be the most preferable sort of theological view *if* all its claims and implications can be sufficiently explained and defended. But there is serious doubt on the part of many philosophers concerning whether this can be done. And in that case, presentism may offer us the best conception of the completeness of God's knowledge. More than a thousand years of discussion have not managed to settle the issue. But in just the last few years, we have succeeded in attaining new levels of clarity concerning what exactly the problem is, what the alternative responses to it might be, and where both their strengths and weaknesses lie.

Certainty and Uncertainty about God's Knowledge

But can we leave this issue so unsettled? If theists can't agree on a solution to the problem of foreknowledge and freedom, then do they share enough beliefs about the knowledge and nature of God (temporal or atemporally eternal) in order for it to be proper to say that they share in common a single idea of God? In preparation for a dispute to be broached in the next chapter, as well as to provide for a perspective on this continuing debate, it is important to raise the question of how much theists can differ in their beliefs and still be talking about the same thing. I think we can see that not only is it legitimate for theists in general, and even Christian theists in particular, to differ about how some divine attributes are to be understood, there is even room for a devout, reflective agnosticism concerning how some such issues are to be settled. There are thus theological matters having to do with the nature of God on which it is not necessary that theists all agree, and on which it is not even necessary that every theist form a specific, detailed belief, in order for it to be true that we believe in and worship the same God.

To see this, let us first recall some features of the method of perfect being theology. We begin with a definition or core concept of God as the greatest possible being. This is the first level of theistic concept building. At this level, our aim is to arrive at a governing focus and to derive, in connection with that focal point, a method for proceeding further along the path of conceptual elaboration. In accordance with the idea of maximal greatness, or perfection, perfect being theology is then developed by means of consulting our value intuitions to determine, at least *prima facie*, which properties are to be considered among the great-making properties constitutive of deity. As our list of properties grows, we begin to consider questions of property grouping, compossibility and comparative, additive value. We also consider which properties are such that their attribution to God would be consistent with all that we independently know about the world.

There is, within the procedure just described so briefly, a differentiation of distinct levels for thinking about the divine. There is, most fundamentally, the core definition of 'God'. Then, by the procedure naturally attached to this definition, a more detailed conception of the overall essence of deity, in its conceptually distinct particulars, is developed. The precise details at this second level are to some extent open to dispute and negotiable within the practice of perfect being theology. Agreement on the first level of conceptual thinking about God is thus compatible with disagreement, and even significant uncertainty, concerning some of the specifications at this second level. And what is true for perfect being theology in this regard is also true for creation theology. There is a first level, core conception and method, and a second level of conceptualizing where there is room for both disagreement and the reserving of judgment. In addition, this is also reflected in the dynamics of using the Bible as a guiding, governing source for our basic conception of God. Agreement that the Bible is of crucial importance for developing our idea of God is compatible with a good deal of disagreement and uncertainty over details of biblical interpretation. There are surely limits for the scope of these disagreements and uncertainties, but our point here is that there is significant room for them to exist as well. And what is true for each of these three methods of thinking about God is true for their joint employment, the composite methodology I have been recommending that we use.

If our idea of God is the idea of a greatest possible creator of all, and we believe this God to be revealed in the documents of the Bible, then we share the same theism regardless of how we might differ on the correct way to understand the completeness of God's knowledge, and even if some of us reserve judgment on the final answer here. We agree that God is perfect, and so we agree that his knowledge is perfect, whatever this might finally amount to. We agree that his knowledge is as complete as it is possible for a state of knowledge to be. And this is agreement on something extraordinary indeed, even if some of the details are yet to be fully resolved.

6

The Being
of God

What sort of a being is God? On the idea of God we have been developing, we have seen that he is conceived of as being such that there is nothing that could possibly detract from his goodness, challenge his power or escape his knowledge. He is an absolutely perfect being, creator of anything which might exist distinct from himself. But, we can sometimes find ourselves asking, what is it *like* to have all these extraordinary attributes? How is the existence of such an individual to be conceived? What mode of existence, or mode of being, could possibly support or allow for such exalted properties?

These are difficult questions, questions which can express a deep perplexity about the existence of God. The sort of God we have been portraying is obviously very different from anything we come across in our normal, physical environment. And he is clearly very different from any of us. His power does not arise from the limited resources of musculature or physical mass. His knowledge is not confined to the storage capacity of a brain. He does not exist in this way at all. He enjoys a transcendent form of existence.

But what does this mean? As we saw in chapter one, there are limits to the sort of transcendence we can ascribe to God. But those limits still allow us to conceive of God as having, fundamentally, a different mode of being from that fragile foothold in reality we know as creaturely existence. In this chapter and the next, we shall explore some austerely metaphysical attributes, properties which are often claimed to be modes of God's being, manners or ways in which he has his other attributes. An understanding of them, and of some of the controversies over them, will help us to grasp, at least to some further extent, the nature of his transcendent being.

Necessity: The Exalted Modality

God is necessarily good. God is necessarily omnipotent. God is necessarily omniscient. Each of these claims can be taken to be the expression of a necessity in more than one sense, as we have seen. They can be understood as expressing necessities *de dicto:*[1]

(1) Necessarily, God is good,
(2) Necessarily, God is omnipotent,
(3) Necessarily, God is omniscient,

where the necessity is, roughly speaking, a conceptual necessity, or a propositional necessity resulting from the unpacking of a concept, the concept of God. In this sense the necessity of God's being good consists in no more than the impossibility of any individual's counting as God, or properly instantiating the concept of God, without that individual's being good. Goodness is a conceptual requirement of deity.

The claims that God is necessarily good, omnipotent and omniscient, can also be understood as the expression of necessities *de re:*

(4) God is necessarily good,
(5) God is necessarily omnipotent,
(6) God is necessarily omniscient,

where the necessity in each case is one holding true of the individual who in fact is God, and is the expression of one of his essential properties, a property without which he could not exist. These *de re* necessities tie goodness, omnipotence and omniscience to the very existence of the divine being. And, as we have noted, the modally most exalted form of perfect being theology will go on to express the even more stringent conceptual requirement of deity that, in order to count as literally divine, an individual must have goodness, omnipotence and omniscience essentially:

(7) Necessarily, God is essentially good,
(8) Necessarily, God is essentially omnipotent,
(9) Necessarily, God is essentially omniscient,

for a being who was ultimately vulnerable to evil, weakness or ignorance in any possible circumstance would not be a greatest possible being.

From this modally exalted conception of the requirements of deity, it follows that any individual who is God has that status essentially. To spell this out most fully, and to extend this idea of deity to the utmost, it will be convenient to employ something like the idea, previously mentioned, of a "possible world." Consider the possible situation of my sitting with a fountain pen in my hand. This possible situation, or possible state of affairs, happens to be actual as I write these words. But there are many states of affairs which are possible but not actual, such as the state of affairs of my having lived my entire life as a rock guitarist, never having taken up philosophy. Now consider the idea of a collection or array of states of affairs, each in itself possible and together compossible. The idea of a possible world is just the idea of a very big collection of states of affairs, as complete an array as is possible. Think of the sum total of all the states of affairs which have been, are and will be included in the entire history of everything that ever exists. Now pause and catch your breath. This is a possible world—the one which happens to have the special status of being actual. But, as philosophers say, there are many other possible worlds which could have been actual instead. There are possible worlds in which I never touch a fountain pen. There are some possible worlds in which I exist and never become a philosopher. So the property of being a philosopher is not one of my essential properties, it is not one of the properties necessary for my existence. I have that property only in some possible worlds, not in all, so we say that I have it *contingently* or *accidentally*.

Many of my properties I have contingently. But some I have *essentially*—in every possible world in which I exist. The property of having a mind, or the related property of being at least potentially conscious, is one of my essential properties. There is no possible world in which I exist utterly devoid of a mind or the potentiality for consciousness.

On the conception of deity we are considering, part of what it means to be God is to have the properties of goodness, omnipotence and omniscience, and to have them essentially. That is to say, it is a conceptual requirement of deity that any individual who is God is God in every possible world in which he exists, and at any and every time at which he might exist. There is no ascending to, or abdicating, this throne. A being whose properties, and ultimate status, were not this stable could not be a greatest possible being.

And we are now in a position to make one further step. Theists who work in the tradition of perfect being theology, and those whose perspective is captured by the precise form of creation theology we have considered want to make one more claim. The further claim is that any individual who is God has this status in and perfectly throughout every possible world. But in order for this to be true, such an individual must of course exist in every possible world. This is what is known as *necessary existence*, the pinnacle of divine necessity. Necessary existence is just existence in all possible circumstances, in all possible worlds. A necessarily existent being is a being whose nonexistence is strictly, metaphysically impossible.

Why have theists endorsed the necessary existence of God? The reasoning from the side of perfect being theology is simple. We live in a world where many things have a very fragile and tenuous existence. Things come to be, things pass away. Many things that could have been never are, and most things that do exist could have failed ever to appear on the stage of reality. We live in a world of contingent beings. But contingency is not the greatest mode of existence imaginable. We can at least conceive of a being who could not possibly cease to exist, whose existence could not have appeared "from nothing," and whose anchorage in reality is so great that it is not even possible for the being to have failed to exist. Surely it is only this necessary existence,

this firmest possible foothold in reality, which is appropriate for a maximally
perfect being. This, in brief, is the argument from perfect being theology.[2]

The reasoning from creation theology is even simpler. If God is thought of
as necessarily the creator, or ultimate cause, of any being which could exist
distinct from himself, in the sense that there is no possible world in which
anything distinct from God exists without deriving its existence from God, it
follows straightforwardly that God must be conceived of as existing in every
possible world. And this is the picture of creation required by any thoroughly
theistic ontology, or world view. Anything less would not portray the ultimate
in creator-creation relations.[3]

So the idea we have before us, from both perfect being theology and creation
theology, is the idea of God as necessarily existent, existent in all possible
worlds, in all possible circumstances. Although this idea connects up so
naturally with both these methods for thinking about deity, it has been a
controversial claim in recent years, yet perhaps not quite as controversial as the
other metaphysical attributes we shall be examining in this chapter and the
next. In each case, however, the controversy among Christian philosophers can
be understood as a disagreement over whether a being characterized as
necessary, or atemporal, or in some other esoterically metaphysical way, can
possibly be the God of the Bible, an utterly free person, creator, sustainer and
savior of all. In each case, an important aspect of the controversy turns on how
different from human beings God can be and still exist as a personal being.

Critics of the claim that God enjoys necessary existence often reason like this.
The most plausible candidates for necessary existence are abstract objects like
numbers, properties and propositions. For try to imagine a possible world in
which nothing exists. If there could be such a world, it would be a world, or
state of affairs, in which the number of things that exist would be properly
numbered by the number 0. The number 0 would be instantiated, or
exemplified, precisely by the absence of anything else. But then *it* would have
to exist to be exemplified, or to number the things that exist. Moreover, it is
one number, so it, itself, would properly be numbered by the number 1, and
so on. In other words, it is impossible that there be a state of affairs or world
in which literally nothing exists. At least the numbers would have to exist in
any world. And the different numbers have different properties, so properties

would have to exist. Likewise, in our attempted specification of a null world, the proposition "Nothing exists" would have to be true; but then, it would have to exist in order to be true of such a circumstance. The net result of such reasoning is that it is plausible to suppose that such abstract objects as numbers, properties and propositions necessarily exist as a sort of formal framework of reality, providing necessary conditions for the possibility of any world. But it is another thing altogether, the critic of divine necessity alleges, to suppose that God exists necessarily. The paradigms of necessary existence, as we have seen, are *abstract objects*. But God is a person, and persons, like tables, chairs and planets, are *concrete objects*. Now, the philosophical distinction between abstract and concrete objects is a difficult one to draw precisely, but the critic here thinks it is clear enough to undermine the belief in God's necessity. For God is surely more like tables, chairs, planets, you and me than he is like numbers, properties and propositions. And we are contingent things.

If God is a person, then indeed in *most* respects he is more like you and me than he is like a number or a property. It just doesn't follow at all that he is unlike numbers and properties in any distinctive respect. In particular, there is no compelling argument here at all for the thesis that God could not exist necessarily unless he were an abstract object. One main distinction between concrete and abstract objects may be that only concrete objects can cause changes in other objects, or initiate causal chains in the world. On this ground, God would clearly stand on the side of concrete objects, regardless of the sweep of his existence across possible worlds. So this form of objection seems to go nowhere.

It may be tempting for critics to argue rather like this: From our experience, we know that

(1) Persons begin to exist and cease to exist.
Thus,
(2) Persons exist contingently.
But
(3) God is a person.
So
(4) God exists contingently.

And thus
(5) God does not exist necessarily.

If a being exists contingently, he exists only in some possible worlds and not in others, thus (5) follows from (4). Theists are committed to (3). Line (2) follows from line (1), in the sense that *if* (1) is true, then (2) is also. But *is* the first premise of this argument something we know to be true from our experience?

We see human persons born. We don't clearly see them begin to exist in any simple, straightforward sense. But if we are Christian theists, we believe that all created human persons begin to exist at one time or another. We see human beings die. We do not see them cease to exist. We see their bodies cease to function. But if we are Christian theists, we believe that all created human persons exist beyond bodily death. In fact, we never know that any intersubjectively experienceable object ceases to exist by sense experience alone. For that sort of knowledge, experience must be supplemented by theory. Otherwise, what seems to be the annihilation of such an object could just be its local disappearance, and it could continue to exist relocated in some other region of space-time. Recognizing this, we must recognize that our experience of human birth and death must be augmented by some theory of human existence before we can draw conclusions about ontological coming-to-be and ceasing-to-be. And the theory of human nature compatible with Christian theology will recognize our contingency as persons only as an implication of the fact that we are *created* persons. So we must judge that, from a theistic perspective, (1) is flawed as it stands, and so is (2). *Created* persons begin to be, and thus created persons exist contingently. But then the conclusions of (4) and (5) would follow only if it could be maintained that, in this sense of contingent creation,

(3') God is a created person,

which is completely contrary to a Christian world-view, and so will be rejected as false. This argument against the necessity of God's existence is thus also a failure.

Some philosophers seem to think that the modalities of necessity, possibility and impossibility always have to do with simple logical consistency or inconsistency. On this view, the proposition that

(G) God exists

could not be a necessary truth, true in all possible worlds, unless

(GN) God does not exist

were somehow formally inconsistent, like

(I) I am both over six feet tall and not over six feet tall,

and impossible for that reason. But I see no good reason to be so restrictive about the grounds of necessity and impossibility. Some critics, like the philosopher J. N. Findlay, have thought that there are no necessities or impossibilities except for those which are established by human linguistic convention or agreement. It is absurd to suppose that the existence of any being in all possible worlds, or even in any world at all, could be a result of some linguistic convention. So, Findlay concludes, the existence of a necessary God is nonsense, an utter impossibility.[4]

Findlay really seems to think that it is *impossible* that there be any necessities or impossibilities not established by or resulting from some convention of linguistic usage. But what convention of linguistic usage establishes this alleged impossibility? None that I know of. Findlay offers no argument for his view that necessity and impossibility can only be the result of linguistic convention. And no one else has succeeded in making such a case. There seems to be no good reason to be restrictive in this way concerning the realm of modality. The theist who endorses the necessity of God's existence has an entirely sensible, and even, as we shall see in the chapter on creation, metaphysically powerful view of necessity and impossibility. Thus, I think it is entirely reasonable to follow the straightforward arguments from both perfect being theology and creation theology for the claim that God exists necessarily in all possible worlds. And, as we shall see, the resultant picture of reality will be one in which it can be said as well that all possible worlds exist in God.

Divine Simplicity

My being is complex in many ways. I exist in an embodied form. I have arms, legs, fingers, toes. I have knowledge, I have emotions. I have desires, hopes, plans, dreams. The power I have to act in the world depends on my mental abilities and the soundness of my body. Consider the property I have of being a philosopher. For many years I lived with no knowledge of philosophy. Through intellectual awakening and hard work I came to exemplify this property, I became a philosopher. But it is a fragile thing and can be lost. A blow to the head, a lack of oxygen to the brain, perhaps an obsessive watching of network television around the clock, could suffice to rob me of this possession, this property so intimately tied to how I think of myself. Even laziness, inattention and simple absorption in the mundane can gradually erode the capacities in which this property resides. What I was, I am not. What I am, I may not continue to be. And what is true of me depends on so many forces outside my control.

Traditionally, many theists have insisted that none of this alterability, fragility or dependency could possibly characterize God. An absolutely perfect creator of all must have what philosophers call *ontological independence*, or *aseity* (existence from his own resources alone, "from himself," hence the Latin *a se*).[5] God cannot be dependent on anything, otherwise he would not be a greatest possible being, and could not be such that everything depends *on him*. He cannot have any sort of complexity involving composition, for wholes composed of parts are dependent upon their parts for what they are. And he cannot have the sort of complexity in his being which would consist in his having his own properties or attributes the way a man or woman has possessions which can be acquired or lost. There must be greater stability and simplicity in the divine being than this.

These reflections have led many theists of the past, and some prominent theists of the present, to endorse a striking metaphysical thesis sometimes known as the *doctrine of divine simplicity*, the claim that, in his innermost being, God must be without any sort of metaphysical complexity whatsoever. This is usually understood to involve a threefold denial:

(1) God is without any spatial parts (the thesis of spatial simplicity),

(2) God is without any temporal parts (the thesis of temporal simplicity), and

(3) God is without the sort of metaphysical complexity which would be involved in his exemplifying numerous different properties ontologically distinct from himself (the thesis of property simplicity).

The thesis of spatial simplicity is endorsed by the vast majority of traditional Christian theists because of considerations deriving from perfect being theology.[6] God is not a physical object, so he does not have physical, or spatially located, parts.

The thesis of temporal simplicity, as we shall see in the next chapter, is endorsed by many theists, but is very controversial, even among Christian philosophers and theologians. This thesis maintains that there is no past, present and future in the life of God, no temporal succession of moments coming to be and passing away. The eternal fullness of divine existence is not divisible into temporal segments as our lives are. God is thus outside of time. We shall temporarily postpone our discussion of this claim until we address the conflict of different interpretations of divine eternity, and at this point shall focus instead on the most controversial thesis contained within the doctrine of divine simplicity—the thesis of property simplicity.

Representative simplicity theorists (those who present the doctrine of divine simplicity as an important part of any theoretically adequate philosophical theology) claim that if God were like us in exemplifying properties distinct from himself, then he would depend on those properties for what he is, in violation of divine aseity. The idea here is a bit difficult to grasp, but it is roughly this: All God's creatures have properties distinct from themselves. I have many, many properties characterizing me, the property of being human, of being male, of being a philosopher, of being from North Carolina, of being a father, of being a pet owner, of loving the ocean, and so on. These are all properties whose existence is distinct from my own. These properties existed and were exemplified by others before I existed, thus they exist distinct from me and do not depend on me for what they are like. But I could not be what I am if it were not for those properties being as they are, so I depend on them for what I am. God cannot depend on anything, so he must not have properties distinct from himself.

Yet we say that God is good, omnipotent, omniscient. We speak of God's properties or attributes, and simplicity itself surely seems to be a property. Should we then think of it as the discrete property of being such as to have no discrete properties? If so, then it seems we have wandered into nonsense unawares. But simplicity theorists have a reply. When we say that God is good, and that God is omnipotent, we are not properly attributing to him ontologically distinct attributes. We are merely conceptualizing the remarkable unity that is God in different ways. According to a main form of the simplicity doctrine, it would be less misleading to say that God is Perfect Goodness, God is Omnipotence, God is Omniscience, where these are understood as identities rather than as the attributions of separate properties. But if these are identities, then it follows by the laws governing identity that Perfect Goodness is Omnipotence, and Omnipotence just is the same thing as Omniscience. Another way to try to put this might be to say that there is only one divine property—Divinity—and it is identical with God. Thus, within the life of God, there is no complexity of properties God has; there is only the one property God is. Simplicity is not the property of having no properties—it is rather a name for the mysterious way in which the being of God supports our many true characterizations of him without ultimately being divisible into substance and attributes, as are his creatures.

With this claim that there is no complexity of properties had by God, we are in deep waters indeed. This is perhaps the most startling, unusual claim ever made about God's being. And it is one with apparently counterintuitive implications. Yet those who endorse it insist that it is of paramount theological importance. It has been thought of as the best explanation for the stability of God's being, his incorporeality, his eternity and his immutability.[7] It has also been presented as the basis for the best view of the relation between God and morality, among other things.[8] But it is an idea whose untoward implications are difficult to defend and whose advantages can perhaps all be had in other ways. It is also an idea whose precise motivation is not so convincing after all, under close scrutiny.

First, as to motivation: What the simplicity theorist is concerned about is that, given the necessary goodness of God, for example, if goodness is thought of as a property distinct from God, then it is true that

(1) If the property of goodness did not exist, then God would not exist.

But this is just an expression of the idea that God's goodness is essential to him—that God is good in every circumstance in which he exists. But since, on the view we have been developing, it is also true that God exists necessarily, in every possible world, it can also be said of the property of goodness that it is essentially such that it is possessed by God. And this can be seen to support the truth of

(2) If God did not exist, then the property of goodness would not exist.

The simplicity theorist thinks that (1) expresses the dependence of God on the property of goodness. But if it did, (2) would express the dependence of the property of goodness on God. But, presumably, ontological dependence, dependence for being or existence, can only go in one direction—if my parents brought me into existence it cannot also be the case that I brought them into existence. Thus, the mere existence and truth of propositions like (1) and (2) cannot alone be taken to show ontological dependence. Their truth merely reflects the logical relation which holds between propositions about necessarily existent entities, and alone implies nothing about the ontological dependence or independence of those entities.

In our chapter on creation, we shall see that a view can be developed in accordance with which any necessarily existent entities distinct from God can be viewed as ontologically dependent on God as the divine, ontologically independent source of all else. If this theistically attractive view is true, it will be impossible to motivate the doctrine of divine simplicity from considerations of aseity alone. Moreover, if the view of divine attributes developed in the previous section of this chapter is correct, other motivations of divine simplicity will be hard to come by. For in the case of God's possession of his defining, distinctively divine attributes, there is no question of coming-to-be and ceasing-to-be. He possesses these properties in all possible circumstances. There is no fragility or tenuousness to his character. His divinity is neither accidental nor temporary. His properties cannot "come apart". The instability and contingency which accompany complexity in our case offer no threat to his exalted status whatsoever. Thus, there is no need to endorse property simplicity to provide for a recognition of God's greatest possible metaphysical stature. The purported benefits of simplicity can be had otherwise.

Finally, there are easily apparent counterintuitive implications of the thesis of property simplicity. First, if God is a property, then either God is an abstract object or some property is a concrete object. Either view seems startlingly counterintuitive, in violation of any standard concrete-abstract distinction. Second, if there is no multiplicity of properties really had by God, it will, I think, be very hard, if not just impossible, to make sense of standard distinctions we make about God. We believe that he is necessarily powerful, but that it is only contingently true of him that he used that power to create our world. He could have created another universe instead, or, perhaps, he could have refrained from creating any physical realm at all. We also believe that it is only contingently, not necessarily, true of God that he called Abram out of Ur, spoke through Moses, and sent the prophets he chose. Moreover, I happen to be wearing a striped shirt today. I could have worn a plain shirt instead. It is a contingent fact that I am garbed in stripes. And God knows this fact. He thus has a belief, or is in a specific state of knowledge, which is contingent. He has the property of being in this cognitive state contingently, since its status must mirror the contingent status of the fact known. God necessarily is a knower. God contingently has the knowledge that I have on a striped shirt. Thus, there is both necessity and contingency with respect to God. And there seems to be no other good way to capture this truth than to say that God has both necessary (essential) and contingent properties. But if that is so, then he cannot "have" just one and only one property, a single property with which he is identical. Nor can he be said to literally have no properties. The thesis of property simplicity therefore must be false.[9]

If one component of the doctrine of divine simplicity is false, the doctrine as a whole is false. Yet it is still possible that the doctrine is an attempt to express a true mystery concerning the real metaphysical unity of God. It is sensible to think there is a special kind of integrity to the being of God. The thesis of property simplicity, as it stands, just fails to capture it. So by rejecting the doctrine of divine simplicity, as presented, I don't mean to be turning my back on any legitimate inklings of divine uniqueness which may ultimately stand behind it. I just mean to indicate that insofar as those inklings can be captured in language, the thesis of property simplicity, and its associated general doctrine, is not what we need for that expression. However, as I have indicated, the thesis of spatial simplicity is widely endorsed by theists, and the thesis of temporal simplicity, while nowadays very controversial, is endorsed by numerous thoughtful theists, and is intimately related to the ideas of divine eternity and immutability, which require discussion in their own right. And it is to them we turn, in the next chapter.

7

God's
Eternity

*G*od is eternal. All theists agree upon that, in *some* sense of the word 'eternal.' That is to say, what all theists agree upon is that there is nothing temporary about the existence and nature of God. Christians add that there is nothing temporary about the promises of God either. And the main content of those promises is often spelled out in terms of salvation into "eternal life" for those who are properly related to God. Yet there are few theists who believe that God will, or even could, endow any of his creatures with exactly the mode of relation to time he has by nature. So in Christian theology it seems that the word 'eternal' is used is at least two ways, perhaps in one sense concerning God, in another concerning the future of those who enjoy a right relationship to him.

But even this is too overly simplified because there are two different and conflicting interpretations of what God's own eternity, or eternality, amounts to. In this chapter, we shall explore what those two interpretations are, and examine many of the arguments which have been given for each as the proper interpretation of God's relation to time. One of the biggest divisions among contemporary theistic philosophers is this difference over how God's eternal mode of existence is to be understood. So a look at the debate is well worth our attention.

The Atemporally Eternal and the Temporally Everlasting

By the claim that God is eternal, many theists mean that God is *everlasting:* He always has existed as God and always will. Some philosophers refer to this as *sempiternity.* It is a *temporal* notion, a conception of God's eternity in terms of time: God's existence is temporally infinite in duration, unbounded in the past and future. On this conception, there is in the life of God a past, present and future, as in the life of his creatures. But unlike any of his creatures, God is everlasting, and necessarily so. His defining attributes—those properties distinctive of deity, i.e., his perfect goodness, omnipotence, omniscience, aseity and so on—he necessarily always has had and always will have. Of course, this is just a consequence of the three claims that

(1) God exists necessarily,
(2) God has all the distinctively divine attributes essentially,
and
(3) God exists in time.

Although the conjunction of these three claims entails an undeniably exalted view of deity, many prominent theists have found this interpretation of eternity inadequate, and have pinpointed claim (3) as the focus of their disagreement.

Such great theists as Augustine, Boethius, Anselm and Aquinas (just to stay with the As and Bs) have insisted on a different and incompatible interpretation of eternity. Theirs is a conception of *timeless* or *atemporal fullness of being.* According to them, God does not in any way exist in time. There is no temporal location or duration in the life of God. He undergoes no temporal succession whatsoever. There is no past, present and future in God's own unique form of existence, or within the divine experience. On this picture, God does not exist throughout the entirety of time; he exists wholly outside of time. The whole temporal realm is a creation of God's and does not contain him as a part. As he transcends space, he also transcends time.

Yet, in lacking temporal duration the life of God suffers from no deficiency. Rather, these theists claim, his atemporality or timelessness provides for the most exalted mode of existence imaginable. In the most famous definition of this aspect of deity ever proposed, Boethius once said, "Eternity is the complete possession all at one of illimitable life."[1] God's eternal present, so to speak, is not immediately lost into an ever-receding past, nor is it the mere anticipation of a still-remote future. There is an unlimited fullness to God's life that does not wait upon the future for its completion or empty itself into the past. This view, according to its adherents, is the most exalted, and only adequate, conception of the ultimacy of God's being.

What we have here, between the temporalists and the atemporalists, is a serious disagreement about the being of God, the mode of his existence. Both camps claim to be talking about the God of the Bible, the greatest possible creator of all. Yet there are no biblical passages which explicitly and undeniably settle the matter. Nor are there arguments from the methodology of either perfect being theology or creation theology which clearly and uncontroversially present the final word on this issue. In order to appreciate the nature of this debate, we need to canvass the main considerations, the arguments and perspectives, which have been taken by their adherents to motivate one or the other of these competing interpretations of eternity. Only by looking, however briefly, at most of the arguments which have been brought forth will we put ourselves into a position to understand the dispute and decide for ourselves how it should be resolved, or whether it can be settled at all. First, we shall examine the considerations raised by atemporalists in favor of their view, laying out each argument in its simplest outlines and mentioning any clear response the temporalists can make. Then we shall reverse the procedure, presenting temporalist arguments and adducing atemporalist responses. In all, eight distinguishable lines of atemporalist argument and four main lines of temporalist thought will be explored.

Atemporalist Arguments

1. *The Simplicity Argument:* The view that God is a being outside time derives ultimately from pre-Christian philosophical sources, such as Plotinus, the Neo-Platonists, and Parmenides. Its main theoretical origination is in the view that

God is metaphysically simple, devoid of any sort of composition or complexity whatsoever. As we have seen in the previous chapter, one component thesis of the doctrine of divine simplicity is the thesis of temporal simplicity, the claim that God is without any temporal parts. This means, roughly, that God's life is not divisible, even in thought, into discrete temporal segments, or stretches of time. This entails that in God there is no *temporal duration*. And if to exist at any moment is to have in one's existence a single temporal part, simplicity specifies also that nothing concerning God's existence has any *temporal location*. But to lack temporal duration and temporal location, and yet to exist, is to exist as an atemporal being. This result is also entailed by the thesis of property simplicity, for if God literally has no properties distinct from himself, he has no temporal properties and thus is outside time.

In the previous section, we have already examined the thesis of property simplicity and found it wanting. So the temporalist can understandably reject this source for an interpretation of eternality. And the thesis of temporal simplicity is too close to being just another statement of the atemporal interpretation of divine eternity to function as an independent motivation or reason for it. But perhaps the original motivation often adduced in support of the thesis of temporal simplicity can be relied upon to deliver the conclusion that God is outside time. Thus, it should be considered.

The argument is based on the claim that any object which has parts is dependent on them in a way in which they are not dependent on it. Since God has the characteristic of aseity, or ontological independence, he cannot be on the receiving end of any such one-way, or asymmetrical, dependence relation. Therefore God cannot have any parts, including temporal parts.

To make clear the claim generating this argument, let us consider some ordinary physical object, such as a clock. A clock depends on its parts in a sense in which they do not depend on it: From the fact that all, or even any, of the parts of the clock are broken, it will follow that the clock is broken, but from the fact that the clock is broken, it will *not* follow that all of the parts of the clock are broken, or perhaps even that any of them is broken—it can just be partially disassembled with crucial parts removed and lost. The parts severally have an integrity not dependent on the integrity of the clock, but the clock itself does not enjoy this lack of dependence on its parts. The truth of the following proposition captures this one-way dependence relation for this case of spatial (physical) parts:

S (1) If all the spatial parts of a clock were to be damaged or destroyed, it would follow that the clock would be damaged or destroyed, but
(2) It is not the case that if the clock were to be damaged or destroyed, it would follow that all its parts would be damaged or destroyed.

Of course, the conditions here could be generalized to give us conditions under which, and presumably under which alone, any spatially composite whole will depend asymmetrically on its parts. If an S-type proposition holds true of every spatially composite whole, then, assuming divine aseity to preclude God's standing on the dependent end of any such asymmetrical relation, it seems to follow that God is not a spatially composite whole.

But now let us apply the same reasoning to the problem of temporal composition. A clock, as an ordinary object, exists in time (otherwise, what good would it be?), and thus can be thought of as having temporal parts. We need to ask whether temporal composition of this sort will always involve an asymmetrical dependence of the whole on its parts. To arrive at an answer, we can just attempt to construct a proposition as similar as possible to S, laying out parallel dependence conditions for the case of temporal composition:

T (1) If all the temporal parts of a clock were to fail to exist, it would follow that the clock would fail to exist, but
(2) It is not the case that if the clock were to fail to exist, it would follow that all its temporal parts would fail to exist.

The problem with T, however, is that, quite simply, it is false. T (1) is true, but the second clause, T (2), is false. So the proposition as a whole is false. If a particular clock were never to have existed, no temporal parts of it would have existed either. This is an interesting difference between temporal parts and spatial (physical) parts. Temporal wholes thus just do not stand in an asymmetric dependence relation to their temporal parts. Thus, it is not at all clear that considerations of divine aseity can be appealed to as a motivation for the thesis of temporal simplicity, or for the atemporal interpretation of the notion of divine eternity.

2. *The Time of Creation Argument:* If God is a temporally everlasting being, then why did he wait so long before creating the world? After all, our universe is only so many billions of years old. What was God doing before he created it? In raising this question, Augustine reports a joke already making the rounds in the fourth century, according to which the answer is: "He was preparing hell for those prying into such deep subjects."[2] But what is the serious philosophical problem here? Presumably, it is felt that if God had existed through infinite time past, prior to his creation of the universe, then there would exist no sufficient reason why he created it exactly when he did rather than earlier, or later for that matter. But it is hard to see the force of this point. For if God is a truly free creator, then he need not have a sufficient reason for every aspect of everything he does. If he wants to create, he is free to arbitrarily pick a time for creation. But why did he wait so long? We can feel this to be a problem: If creating our world was a good thing, and God is in time, then why indeed would he have delayed so long (infinitely long) before doing this good deed?

First, it is not as if this problem could not have been raised if God had acted much, much earlier than he did in creating the world. For any act of creation by an everlasting being would be preceded by infinite time. But the atemporalist may insist that this is precisely the point. On a temporal conception of divine eternity, this question is unavoidable. The atemporalist avoids it altogether by claiming that there was no time of the creation act at all—God eternally wills that there come into existence a physical universe, a space-time before which there was no time. So there can be no worry about a divine delay.

But the worrisomeness of the alleged delay is surely dealt with to some extent by the possibility that God has always, or very frequently (to put it mildly) been creating and bringing into existence good things prior to the creation of our universe. Nothing in the Bible or in the fundamentals of Christian faith requires us to hold that the bringing about of our universe is the only creative endeavor in which God has ever engaged. Thus, we need not live with the specter of an infinite delay in God's creative impulses, if we endorse the temporal interpretation of divine eternity.

3. *The Nature of Time Argument:* Time, it has been suggested by many theorists, is just a measure of the existence of physical objects, and as such is just an aspect, or dimension of the space-time manifold which is the formal, relational structure of the existence of our physical universe. Moreover, there is no absolute time, no moving NOW which stretches across the entirety of the universe, no universal simultaneity for events at a time. Simultaneity and temporal flow are relative to the movements of physical systems and to the placement of observers in those physical systems. But God is not a physical object, nor is he physically present in any physical system. As a knower, he is not the sort of observer dependent upon physical signals for his acquisition of knowledge. Because of the nature of time and the nature of God, God cannot sensibly be said to be in time at all.

This cluster of considerations, which derive from a contemporary understanding of the nature of time, as viewed within physics and cosmology, has been thought by many philosophers to be decisive. Atemporalists have drawn upon such considerations to formulate questions that they have considered unanswerable, and embarrassing, for temporalists, like: "What time is it for God?" or "Exactly *where* is God's present moment, God's NOW?"

But to these considerations, the temporalist has a response. Let us grant that God is not a physical object—that is, let us assume that God is not spatially located as an object within any physical system and does not depend upon physical signals for his knowledge. At most, what will follow from this is that his existence and experience are not confined by any of the restrictions due only to the limitations of a particular physical time-frame. As omnipresent and omniscient, God has access to every physical time-frame and to the relations of simultaneity and nonsimultaneity within all creaturely time-frames, yet God's own existence is not rooted in any particular one of them. To say that God is a temporal being is not to say that he exists within the bounds of Eastern Standard Time or Daylight Savings Time. It is only to say that he is a being whose life encompasses successive states. He is aware of one earthly development, and then he is aware of the next. He speaks to Abram, and then later he speaks to Moses. He sends his Son, becoming incarnate in the world, and later he pours out his Spirit. He creates and then he saves. This is sequence and succession. If it is succession *within* the life of God, God is a temporal being, even without the regularity of event and the limitation of framework which characterizes the temporality of physical systems in our universe. Thus, the considerations from the nature of *physical* time do not block the belief that God is a temporal being, they only constrain the way in which that belief is to be understood.

4. *The Nature of Infinity:* There is an argument against the possibility of what is often called a "realized infinity" or an actually existent infinite series. And if this is a good argument, it is an argument against God's having existed for an actually infinite number of past times of finite duration. The core of the argument is quite simple and is based on the following consideration: Begin any successive process of adding or producing finite elements; for example, begin counting—1, 2, 3, 4, 5, 6 and so on. The number series is said to be infinite, and so, supposing that you yourself are everlasting in the future direction and have an amazing tolerance for boring tasks, you could keep counting without end. But there will never come a time, despite the infinity of the counting numbers and your own infinite persistence, when you will have succeeded in naming infinitely many numbers. There can therefore never be a completed infinity. To characterize something as infinite is to characterize its *potential* as open-ended or unbounded, and that is all. There can be no realized infinity of successively actualized tasks or events, and so in this sense there can be no such actually existent infinite series of any kind. Thus, the application of this reasoning concludes there cannot have been up until now an infinite series of events which have occurred in the life of God. He cannot have succeeded in existing through an infinite number of finite spans of time, as the temporal interpretation of eternity requires. Therefore, his eternity must consist in atemporal existence.

But the temporalist can offer a quick reply to this argument. It is clear that there cannot ever be a realization of an additive, infinite succession *which has a beginning*. But God's existence from all eternity past is not the sort of series or succession which has a beginning. God necessarily lacks a beginning. This is something that all parties to this dispute agree upon. Thus, it is not the case that, on the temporalist view, God is the sort of being to whom this sort of argument clearly applies. Perhaps other arguments from the nature of infinity can be devised to block the claim that God is temporally everlasting, but it is difficult to imagine the shape they will have to take if they are to be persuasive.[3]

5. *The Immutability Argument:* Some atemporalists have argued that in order to be perfect, or in order to be the sort of creator whose perfect activity can be the explanation of all else, God must be utterly changeless, and absolutely incapable of undergoing any sort of change whatsoever. But without change of any kind there is no time. Thus, God's existence cannot be enmeshed in the temporal web.

There are actually two sorts of reasoning involved here. First, it has been claimed by numerous theists that God cannot change, because all change is either change for the better or change for the worse. But God is necessarily a greatest possible being. So he cannot change for the better, since if he did, he would not have been the greatest possible being prior to the change. And he cannot change for the worse, since if he did, he would not be the greatest possible being subsequent to the change. Therefore, God cannot change.

But why think that all possible changes are changes in value? Can't there be value-neutral changes? As I write this sentence I change from forming one letter to forming the next, but I see no reason to think that such changes necessitate an increase or a decrease in my intrinsic value or metaphysical stature at all. And if there are value-neutral changes, it will not follow from the fact that God cannot change for the better or for the worse that God cannot change at all. So his perfection does not clearly motivate a doctrine of absolute immutability after all.

Some philosophers have suggested that in order for the existence and activity of God to serve as the proper stopping point for an ultimate explanation of the existence and activity of all else, of all the inventory of our changing universe, God himself must be utterly devoid of change in any respect. Otherwise, the argument goes, those changes in God would themselves require further explanation and we would not have arrived at a proper stopping-point for all explanation. The suggestion is that only if God's activity is altogether timelessly eternal and unchanging in every respect will there exist an ultimate and complete theistic explanation of everything.

If every change attributable to God—such as the transition from not yet creating our world to saying "Let there be light," or the changes from speaking to Moses to no longer engaging in that communication—if every such change required explanation in terms of something other than God and his free choices or if all free choices required explanation, then a problem might indeed exist here. But a temporalist can insist that no acceptable general principle of explanation—for instance, no plausible version of what theists have called "the principle of sufficient reason"—will demand of every free choice that it have an independent explanation. Genuine freedom involves the ability to act without a sufficient reason for the details and timing of one's act. For some of God's actions, there may be sufficient reasons, or necessitating explanations having to do with the nature, character or desires of God, but for some of God's actions there need be no such explanation. Those changes consisting in actions which have an explanation will have it internal to God, and those which do not have such an explanation do not require any other. And, furthermore, any changes on the side of God arising merely out of his relations to changing creatures will themselves be traceable in one way or another to the free will with which God has endowed those creatures, and thus indirectly to his free act of endowment, or more directly to a creative choice of God's. In any case, all the theoretical explanation for what there is and for what there occurs which is compatible with freedom, divine and creaturely, will be had, and there will be a proper theistic stopping-point to explanation without its being postulated that God is outside time.

6. *The Pure Act Argument:* Following Thomas Aquinas, many theists have suggested that in God there can be no unactualized potential. God is thus referred to as "Pure Act," in whom there is no becoming. But all change and temporal progression is a form of becoming. Therefore, God cannot exist as the sort of being who progresses through successive moments of time.

This is basically just a variant on the perfection argument for absolute immutability. If all potential were potential for additive value, potential from whose realization would accrue new increments of intrinsic value, or perfection, then this would be a persuasive line of argument. But if there is potentiality which is value-neutral with respect to intrinsic value, or metaphysical stature, this argument does not go through. For God's absolute perfection requires only that he not engage in or undergo becoming which adds to or detracts from his intrinsic value. No other becoming is clearly ruled out by his perfection. And it certainly seems that the sort of becoming which consists in no more than being a temporal individual living through successive states of existence does not alone threaten the requirements of perfection, as understood from the perspective of the Christian faith.

7. *The Omniscience and Freedom Argument:* As we have seen in chapter five, many people have thought that the existence of complete, infallible, divine foreknowledge of the future is difficult to reconcile with the existence of genuine creaturely freedom. And some have thought that this problem has a bite only if God is thought of as existing *in time* and thus as literally having infallible beliefs about our actions *before* we perform them. The suggestion is that the problem will be lessened, or circumvented entirely, if God is conceived of rather as existing atemporally and as seeing all of history in one sweeping "eternal present." We have already examined what is problematic about this suggestion. It is not obvious at all that a mere postulation of timelessness will alone deal with the problem that a complete omniscience can raise for free will. But, as I have pointed out, a Molinist perspective on divine knowledge can be combined with an atemporalist picture to yield interesting results. Yet, it is far from clear that any such consideration alone could be enough to motivate a view of timelessness.

8. *The Perfection Argument:* There is one more noteworthy line of reasoning, however, which we should consider very seriously. The atemporalist can argue that if God were in time, he would lack a certain value, or state of value, that a timelessly eternal existence would capture. But if God is a greatest possible being, he cannot lack any important value-making characteristic consistent with his other properties. Atemporal eternality is such a characteristic. Therefore, God must exist outside time.

This argument, of course, turns on the claim that it would be better for God to enjoy a timelessly eternal existence than for him to be an everlasting temporal being. Why? Well, consider the vicissitudes of temporal existence. My own experience of my children, Sara and Matthew, as infants and toddlers was a wonderful thing. My experience of them as schoolchildren is wonderful as well, but it is a gift purchased at a price: I no longer experience them as newborns, or as crawlers first exploring the world. I can remember those times, but I can no longer live them. They are past, continually receding farther from my grasp. I'm sure that my experience of them as adults is capable of far surpassing anything I can now imagine. But at that time I'll no longer have the joys of living with them as six and eight year olds. Time carries away things of great value. It also bears new values, but those too must quickly pass away. Wouldn't it be wonderful if all the joys of the present and the future could be experienced without ever relinquishing any to a past which is beyond the reach of immediate awareness? The fact that our joys are ephemeral is a function of, an aspect of, the fact that we are imperfect. Surely, it would be better for a being capable of love, appreciation and enjoyment never to suffer loss. So, surely, a greatest possible being, a perfect being such as God, should not be thought of as undergoing the sort of loss necessarily involved with being temporal. God, therefore, must exist outside of or "above" time, eternally relating equally to every thing, person and event swept along by the river of time. For anyone stung by the bittersweet evanescence of temporality, this is a psychologically powerful line of argument. Many of us do naturally, intuitively endorse this suggestion: if it is possible for God, with his other properties, to be so related to this world, it would be better for him to be. It would be a more perfect form of existence. But *is* it possible? More specifically, is it possible for a being with God's other properties, is it possible for the God of the Bible, to exist in this way? At this point the temporalists bring forth their arguments, arguments that it is not possible, and thus that the greatest form of existence, the mode of being possessed by God, is after all that of being temporally everlasting. And so to these arguments we now turn.

Temporalist Arguments

1. *The Temporal Action Argument:* One of the most common lines of reasoning among temporalists goes like this. The God of the Bible is an agent, the primary actor in a historical drama. He created the world, brought about human existence, and then began a history of interaction with his human creatures. He spoke through one prophet, then another, finally incarnating himself as a human being, sending his Spirit, and calling individuals into closer union with himself. He is a God who responds to human needs. But, the argument then maintains, a timeless, atemporal being could not be involved in this way in temporal action, action within the realm of temporal history. For an atemporal being never changes, and the sort of actions ascribed to the

biblical God require that he be doing one thing at one time (creating), and something else at a later time (calling Abram), and yet again something different at a still later time (speaking to Moses). A being who does different things at different times is a being in time. Thus, God's eternity must be understood to be one of everlasting temporal duration.

Atemporalists have no difficulty in responding to this popular form of argument. We must first draw a careful distinction between an action and its effects. Suppose, for example, that in the middle of the night I hear a noise which awakens me. Rising from bed, I reach over and flip on a switch for the downstairs light. The light wakes the dog, frightens the prowler, and alerts a policeman driving past to potential trouble. How many actions have I performed? A few philosophers, referred to as "multipliers," say "at least five":

(1) I flipped the switch.
(2) I turned on the light.
(3) I woke the dog.
(4) I frightened the prowler.
(5) I alerted the policeman.

But was I really that busy in the middle of the night, performing so many distinct actions? A more intuitive approach, taken by those known as "unifiers" says no: I performed only one action, say, that of flipping the switch, which had many effects, such as the light's coming on, the dog's waking, etc. But this intuitively appealing distinction between an act and its effects is all we need for an understanding of how an atemporal God could act at different times, in different ways, while never himself changing. The story is simple: There is one eternal divine act outside of time that has a great number of different effects in time, at different times. One effect of this eternal divine act is the world's coming into being. Another is Abram's hearing certain words at a particular time. Still another effect of this same act is Moses' hearing of different words at a later time, and so forth. The single eternal act of God has a bewildering variety of effects with respect to his temporal creation. But from the evident truth that those effects take place at different times, it may not legitimately be inferred that they are effects of distinct actions which also take place at different times.

This move does seem to block the argument as presented, but it admittedly results in a highly unusual picture of divine action, fairly distant from anything the ordinary believer typically entertains. All actions ever truly ascribed to God are just manifestations in time of one atemporal act. Overwhelming. However, in the world in which we live, it seems that any ultimate, theoretical account of anything will depart fairly dramatically from the unreflective opinions of us ordinary laymen.

But some philosophers have worried that even if this conception of God's action will allow an atemporal being to act into this temporal world, it will not allow for a convincing picture of God's acting *in response* to creaturely developments, creaturely needs and creaturely requests. The Old Testament presents many dialogues between God and human beings. Can any true dialogue be held between an atemporal and a temporal being? It seems not, for dialogue seems to require an initial remark or request to be *followed by* a response to that initiative, which *in turn* elicits a later contribution, and so on.

This, however, is really no separate problem at all. A response is just an action or utterance performed in the light of, because of, and in answer to some distinct action or utterance. It may even be part of our ordinary concept of a response that an event which is a response must be experienced subsequent to the experience of the event to which it is a response, if it is to be received *as* a response. But, given the distinction drawn between actions and their effects, what blocks the atemporalist from specifying that God timelessly wills that in response to a request which he eternally knows is to be made by Moses at time t, a voice will be heard by Moses at $t + 1$, responding to the request? The appointed words are intended for Moses in the light of, because of, and in answer to his request. They are heard subsequent to his making of the request. In what way is this not acceptable as a model of divine responsiveness?

The main problem, of course, is that we immediately find ourselves once again facing up to the perplexing question of how a timeless God could have complete knowledge of our worldly futures, and yet our actions in these futures be free. The conception of God as an atemporal agent acting into a temporal world such as ours carries the cost of having to defend something like the Molinist conception of divine knowledge and human freedom we have explored in chapter five. And so this conception of God's being is held hostage to the problems and unresolved issues attending that distinct idea. A temporalist conception of God's eternity is compatible with an openness concerning the future free acts of God's creatures which many theologians and philosophers find attractive. On a temporalist view, one does not have to conceive of God's all-at-once seeing to it that all divine interventions into the temporal order are, so to speak, predetermined as effects appropriately timed so as to dovetail naturally into the eternally known free decisions of his creatures.

2. *The Insufficiency Argument:* This is basically the simple contention that none of the atemporalist motivations or arguments for divine timelessness succeeds in compelling a theist to adopt that view of God's relation to time, coupled with the general principle that whenever allowed to choose between the more bizarre and the less bizarre as an explanation or account of anything, one should adopt the less bizarre, contemporary physics notwithstanding. A difference should make a difference. And the bigger the difference in what is postulated, the bigger a difference it should make in what can be explained or accounted for. Where is the big difference made by positing something so unusual as divine timelessness? Another way of putting the same, or at least a similar, point, would be to say that the more esoteric theoretical commitments, not independently known or plausibly believed to be true, which are needed to support a given interpretation or account of a phenomenon, the more vulnerable and less warranted that interpretation or account is. Now, all Christian theists of any traditional bent acknowledge that God is personal, or a person. Deity encompasses personhood and personal agency. But the account of God as a timeless person, an atemporal agent, requires more unusual suppositions, and a more complex theoretical framework to support it (the apparatus of middle knowledge, etc.) than the conception of God as temporal. Therefore, all else being about equal, this more esoteric interpretation should be eschewed in favor of a more sensible interpretation of divinity as temporally everlasting.

This principle, or type of principle, is in general a good one. What the atemporalist is more likely to contest is the judgment that all those considerations traditionally marshalled to support timelessness are insufficiently persuasive. Not *one* of the eight arguments surveyed has enough impact? This is what the atemporalist will ask, and it is a conclusion he will typically deny. But to evaluate that response we can usually do no more than go back over each of the arguments for atemporality and their criticisms. Another temporalist strategy at this point is often to try to highlight *how* unusual elements of the whole theory are. For example, if the claim of timelessness is embedded in a more general theory of divine simplicity, the temporalist will hammer on its problems. If God is identical with his one eternal act, and it contingently has the effects it has, then God could have existed as identical with that same act, and yet it resulted in no world at all, or some very different universe instead. But how could this be, if it is the very same act, and there are no independent causal mechanisms through which it has its effects? These and other troubling questions can make inquirers quite wary of buying into such an extreme view on the relation of God to time. But they certainly do not amount to refutations of timelessness.

3. *The Biblical Interpretation Argument:* In the Bible, God is represented not only as carrying on conversations but as "walking in the cool of the Garden" near Adam and Eve. He is said to engage in actions of remembering and, for our sakes, forgetting. He seems really to suffer over the errant ways of his creatures. But surely, temporalists insist, these are activities which take time and take place in time. So God is in time.

The atemporalist rebuttal is quick. We do not attribute to God a mouth on account of the fact that he spoke to Moses, or feet because he was said to walk in the Garden. We cannot and do not read these passages so anthropomorphically. God did not talk metaphysics with the biblical authors, nor was their purpose in writing that of teaching the particulars of philosophical theology. They wrote so as to be understood by the average person, and they sought to convey to us primarily what God has done for us and how we should respond. Clearly, once we recognize this, we must admit that we should be extremely cautious about drawing metaphysical conclusions concerning the being of God from vivid or pictorial representations of how God has dealt with his people in the Bible.

Moreover, there are biblical passages which are not so anthropomorphic, and which can be taken to point in the other, atemporal direction. For instance, we read in 2 Peter 3:8 that "with the Lord one day is as a thousand years, and a thousand years as one day," which, if not to be taken quite literally, at least seems to point away from the existence of God being a normal, temporal existence. This can be, and has been, taken by readers to be a poetic indication that God is in fact outside the categories of time. And then there is Malachi 3:6—"I am the Lord; I do not change." If this can be taken absolutely strictly as a piece of metaphysics, and God does not change in even the most minimal sense of existing from one time to another, then this passage presents God as atemporal. But, unfortunately, what we have in this passage is not clearly the metaphysics of God's relation to time. It is rather a reassurance of the stability of God's moral character and his intentions toward his people.

The most natural reading of most biblical texts about God is one on which God is seen as a temporal being. He is talked about in temporal language and there is not any clear nonpoetic passage to the contrary. But, as we have indicated, it is very difficult to resolve a disputed point concerning a fairly esoteric matter in theistic metaphysics by just consulting biblical passages. As they were written for very different purposes, their content will often fail to settle such an issue.

4. *The Argument from Change and Knowledge:* In the Bible, God does seem to change from doing one thing at one time to doing another thing at a later time. We have already seen how the atemporalist can distinguish between an act and its effects in such a way as to deflect the implication that God is ever-changing as an actor. It is not quite so easy to maintain that God is never-changing as a knower. Our world is clearly an ever-changing realm of becoming. God's existence is supposed to be a never-changing realm of being. But then how can a never-changing God have perfect knowledge of an ever-changing world? Surely God's perfect acquaintance with his creation requires an ever-changing awareness on his part as to what is happening, *as it happens.* In brief, the suggestion is that God's relation to a changing world implicates him in change as well. But change requires time. In every case in which an object undergoes change, it comes to lack at some time a property it had at an earlier time, or it gains a property it lacked at a prior time. In either case, an object must exist through different times in order to change. Therefore, as a being whose relation to the world implicates him in change, God must be

thought of as dwelling in time as well.

In response to this and similar arguments, atemporalists often draw a distinction between real change and merely relational change, which is to be understood as no real change at all. The distinction is usually made in something like the following way. Suppose that unknown to me, there is a dog lying down, exactly a mile to my right, and that suddenly he gets up and walks away. Because of his move, I apparently come to lack a property I earlier had— the property of having a dog exactly one mile to my right. Yet, have I undergone any sort of real change? Has there been a change *in me*? Surely not. It was not I who underwent any sort of real change in this story, but the dog who got up and walked away. In fact, many philosophers will refuse to acknowledge in this story that I change properties in any sense at all. It is true at one time that there is a dog one mile from me, and false at a later time that this situation exists. Perhaps, they suggest, such a change is not to be registered by attributing to me properties, or the losing of properties, at all. If there is any sense in which I can be said to have undergone a change in this story, it is no more than a merely relational change, and thus is no real change whatsoever.

Try another story. Suppose Percy dreams of vanilla ice cream daily for a long time. But then at some point he suddenly ceases to have this dream, and dreams of strawberry ice cream instead. Does the flavor vanilla lose a property it once had—the property of being the ice cream of Percy's dreams? And does strawberry gain that property? Surely, any real change here is not in the flavors vanilla and strawberry, but rather in Percy, in his dreams. The only sense in which the ice cream flavors can be said to have undergone a change is in the loose and nonliteral sense of merely relational change.

Atemporalists use this sort of distinction to explain away any appearance of change in God. When God created the world, God underwent no real change at all. It merely began to be true that the world existed. And when God began to speak to Abram, again, God did not suddenly gain properties he lacked before, only Abram really changed from a state of not hearing God speak to one of now hearing the divine call. Likewise, God's awareness of the golden calf did not arise as he saw its being built. He eternally knew that it was being built at a certain time. The change of its coming to be built was not reflected in a change in God's knowledge. All change, all real change, is change on the side of the world, not in God's state of being. The only sense in which God can be said to undergo change, and this is no real change at all, is in the loose and nonliteral sense of merely relational change.

But this denial of all change on the side of God turns on the applicability of the real change/merely relational change distinction to the relationship that obtains between God and his changing world. And there are reasons to doubt the plausibility of its application here. To see this, consider one more standard sort of story of merely relational change. A woman's husband is on a diplomatic trip to a foreign land and, unknown to her, dies at the hands of a terrorist. At the moment of his death, she becomes a widow. But at that time, we can suppose that the change she undergoes is a merely relational change. The circumstances involve so far no real changes on her part. Contrast this with an alternate story in which the murder occurs in her presence, or an even worse variant in which she herself pulls the trigger. In neither of these cases is her becoming a widow a set of circumstances involving only merely relational change on her part. In light of this difference, we can isolate at least three features of any situation in which one object can be described as having undergone no more than merely relational change, logically reflecting some real change in a different object. First, the ongoing existence of the really changing object and its having at least most of the nonrelational properties it has are matters in some sense causally and metaphysically independent of the object undergoing the merely relational change. Second, the real change in question involves no occurrent exercise of power on part of the object undergoing the merely relational change. And third, the real change is not registered as a piece of knowledge or belief on the part of the individual going through merely relational change.

In each of the stories presented to illustrate clearly a case of merely relational change (the dog, the ice cream and the unknowing widow), all three of these features are present. But these are features which could never hold true of God and any of his creatures, such that the creature underwent real change and God did not. As we shall see in the next chapter, it is a firmly entrenched theistic belief that each of God's creatures depends on God moment to moment for its existence. Nothing can exist causally or metaphysically independent of God.

Further, nothing can happen without at least the concurrent operation of God's conserving power. And, most importantly, nothing can happen without God's knowing it. Whenever we have a plausible case of real change in one object reflected in merely relational change on the part of another, we have an object undergoing the latter which exists in numerous forms of isolation from the object going through the former. It is impossible for God to exist in such isolation from his creatures that exist. Therefore, it is hard to see how the atemporalist can plausibly claim that in knowing and relating himself to an ever-changing world, God himself never experiences any real change, but at most can be said to undergo the merely relational change, which is no genuine change at all. But if that is so, it is hard to see how the God of this world can exist outside of time.

There are ways around this argument. The three features we have identified can be claimed to be inessential to cases of merely relational change. But this strikes me as implausible. It is, though, a move that can be made. And it can block this argument. There are ways of blocking, answering or avoiding every argument we have looked at, both for the atemporal perspective and for the temporalist alternative. But some of the considerations we have raised clearly embody insight and must carry some weight in our reflection on this difficult topic. I think one thing we can see from all this is that an atemporal interpretation of eternity which seeks to remain sensitive to the biblical revelation, as well as a sophisticated temporalist understanding of eternity, are both philosophical views which can be held and defended by a Christian seeking to articulate a reasonable idea of God. God will be ascribed the most perfect relation to time compatible with all the constraints we have considered. In particular, he will be ascribed the greatest relation to temporality compatible with his being the creator of this world, whichever relation that might be. As long as we can agree upon that, we can even remain agnostic on how this issue is to be settled. If we do reserve judgment here, our idea of God will not be complete, but completeness is anyway more than we can hope for with respect to an idea *of God*. Even with this issue unresolved, so long as we maintain tight constraints on the kind of resolution we will allow, we can still be said to hold, however incompletely, a determinate idea of God.

8

The
Creation

*T*he majestic introduction to the book of Genesis proclaims that

In the beginning, God created the heavens and the earth.[1]

This is the key to a distinctively theistic perspective on reality. This one statement captures the heart of a theistic world-view We live in a created universe. For centuries, theists have held that the single most important truth about our world is that it is a created world. And it is no exaggeration to add that it is one of the most important truths about God that he is the creator of this world.

Aquinas once expressed the core of the doctrine of creation quite succinctly with the single sentence:[2]

Anything that exists in any way must necessarily have its origin from God.

The philosophical view which is here so crisply and simply conveyed, I shall refer to as the *metaphysical doctrine of creation*. I understand it as a thesis about the metaphysical or ontological dependence of all things distinct from God on God as their source of being, the ultimate cause of their existence.

As a philosophical thesis, the metaphysical doctrine of creation is not to be thought of as necessarily allied to, or as in competition with, any particular scientific theory of physical cosmology or biological development. A few years ago many religious people enthusiastically welcomed and loudly endorsed what is popularly known as the *Big Bang theory of physical cosmology*. The physical singularity which was postulated to have issued in an almost inconceivable, explosive origination of our current cosmos was widely baptized as a scientific acknowledgment of the act of divine creation. But, as many physical cosmologists were quick to point out, the postulation of the Big Bang is not at all the same thing as the acknowledgment of an absolute origination of all things physical from some nonphysical, divine source. The theorized explosion is compatible with an oscillating universe cosmology, according to which, on a colossal time scale, there are repetitive cycles of explosion, expansion, equilibrium and contraction, resulting in a further explosion, and so forth. An intelligent person can accept a Big Bang cosmology without endorsing any form of divine creation, or can adopt the metaphysical doctrine of creation without any commitment to the hypothesized Big Bang. A theist might, for example, endorse some form of the alternative tale told by recent plasma physics instead. Physics is not metaphysics. So in order to understand the theistic doctrine of creation, it is important to keep these two enterprises of human intellectual explanation distinct.

Nor is the metaphysical doctrine of creation alone to be viewed as a determinant of biological theory. In recent years, there have been pitched courtroom battles and skirmishes in the popular press between people widely known as *creationists* and others, called by the creationists *evolutionists*. However this ongoing debate is to be understood, it is not a debate in metaphysics, or in basic philosophical theology. Within the world of serious religious believers, there are both theistic creationists and theistic evolutionists in the battle over developmental biology. Biology is not metaphysics.

Our concern in this chapter with the doctrine of creation will be entirely a concern with the fundamental metaphysical and philosophical issues faced by any traditional theist, however he might appraise current theories of physical cosmology and biological development. We are seeking a level of understanding distinct from that promised by any application of the methods of the natural sciences. And our focus will be not so much on the natural world itself as on some of what can be learned about God by reflecting on the metaphysical doctrine that he is its creator, the ultimate source of its existence.

The Nature of Creation

In order to grasp what it means for God to be the world's creator, we need to examine what has been said about the act of divine creation, the nature of the activity itself, as well as about the dependence of God's creatures on him which results from that activity. It will be natural to begin with a consideration of God's activity of creating.

It is often said that divine creation is an activity which is completely free, rational and good. A variety of things can be and usually are meant by this threefold characterization. I believe we can explicate them best by considering these three characteristics in reverse order. We shall thus explore first what is meant by the goodness of divine creation, then its rationality, and finally, its freedom. This will be a proper ordering of our examination due to the fact that, as will become clear, the goodness of creation informs its rationality, and both together structure its freedom.

As we have seen in chapter three, God is conceived of traditionally as a perfectly good being. And as we shall see, a perfectly good being's character can be expected to be manifested in his actions. Now, it is easy to see that the fundamental activity of creation, as performed by God, is the most basic *giving of being*. Human creation, by contrast, involves a *using of being* in novel ways. Any act of creation on the part of a creature presupposes the existence of things not brought into existence by that creative agent. Creaturely creation thus works with what is already given. Divine creation is more thoroughgoing, and is not to be thought of as an operation performed upon something already existing. And since this most basic giving of being is thought to be the province of God alone, this sort of creation can be thought of as the most distinctly divine activity. As such, then, it should manifest God's goodness if anything does. It should be good. And, appropriately, from early on in the book of Genesis, we are told that God surveyed the products of his creative acts and saw that they were good, very good.[3]

But here we run up against what can be thought to be a philosophical problem. We expect any act of divine creation to be a good act. And it seems natural to suppose that no act of creation can be good unless its product, what is created, is itself also good. For good gives rise to good. But this is where the problem arises. If God is the greatest possible being, no act of creation can result in anything greater. It is just impossible that anything be greater than a greatest possible being. Now, consider our universe as God's creation, the product of his creating activity. Either the universe has positive value or it doesn't. But if it does have positive value, then it seems we are forced to admit that *God plus the universe* is greater than *God alone*. For if God manifests some positive level of value *n* and the universe manifests at least a single unit of positive value, 1, then the additive value of God plus the universe is at least *n* + 1, which is greater than *n*. But it is impossible that anything be greater than God, so it is impossible that the universe have positive value.

This, however, seems to leave us with something equally unacceptable. For if the created universe has no positive value whatsoever, then nothing in it has positive value. If parts of the universe had value, then, as the sum of its parts, the universe would have positive value. But if nothing in the universe has value, human life has no value. Nor could God have been right when he gazed upon various items in creation and perceived them to be good. But these conclusions are totally unacceptable from a Christian, or traditionally theistic, point of view. It is impossible that God be wrong in his perceptions or judgments and, as created in God's image, human beings must be of value. Furthermore, if nothing in the universe has any positive value, what reason could God possibly have had to create it?

Either the universe has value or it doesn't. There is no third option. But either supposition seems to get us into trouble, yielding, as it does, some impossibility or other. We thus seem to be faced here with a true dilemma. Let us refer to it as the *dilemma of created goodness*. Some such line of reasoning has troubled many people who have reflected on the nature of creation. Fortunately, however, it is a problem that is easy to solve.

We must first clearly distinguish between a being, an entity, an individual, on the one hand, and any *state of affairs* which involves that individual. The distinction is a fundamental and quite simple one. I am an individual being, my Pelikan 800 fountain pen is an individual entity, and we are both involved in the state of affairs of *my writing this sentence with my Pelikan 800 fountain pen.* Likewise, we must carefully distinguish between the state of affairs of that fountain pen's existing and the object which is that fountain pen.

With this sort of distinction clearly in mind, we can clarify exactly what the central claim of perfect being theology is: It is that God is to be thought of as the greatest possible *being.* And this is a claim that does not entail the separate proposition that the state of affairs of God's existing alone is the greatest possible state of affairs. The latter proposition is one that the Anselmian theist can deny. And it is one which the Christian theist will deny. Following the affirmations of the book of Genesis, and in accordance with some metaphysical or axiological principles connecting the goodness of God with the goodness of his creation, we can acknowledge that the state of affairs consisting in God's sharing existence with our created universe is greater than the state of affairs of God's existing in pristine isolation or solitude. But from this, it does not follow that there is any being or individual greater than God. This would be the case only if God and the created universe could be thought of as parts of a larger object, God-and-the-world, which could be assigned a value as a distinct individual, additively derived from the values of its parts. And this is prohibited for at least two reasons. First, there is no natural principle of unity in accordance with which God and the created universe would together compose one object.[4] Second, it is just conceptually precluded by perfect being theology that God ever be considered a part of a larger and more valuable whole, an entity distinct from, but partially composed by, God. With all this in mind, we can affirm the positive value, even the great positive value, of the created universe, without thereby posing any threat to the conception of God as the greatest possible being, and without any risk of contradiction arising in connection with that conception. With sufficient care in our thought about God and creation, the dilemma of created goodness does not arise at all.

In creating our universe, God brought into existence goodness, or value, that he was not obligated to bring into existence. In creating, he brought into existence good things, valuable things, which need not have existed. As productive of good, and as intentionally productive of good, the activity of creation itself is good.

What is it for creation to be rational? Part of what theologians and philosophers mean to convey when they characterize creation as rational is that it is *thoroughly intentional* in character. There is nothing "blind" about divine creation. God does not say "let there be something or other" and then look to see what has come into being. He is, rather, thoroughly superintendent over all the details of creation. There is nothing inadvertent or unintentional in God's bringing into existence being.

Further, it is part of the rationality of creation that it is *purposive.* It is directed toward some goal perceived to be of value. In particular, God creates in order to share his being and share his glory. What he creates, he creates to that end. Of course, in order to be rational, it is not enough that an activity be goal-directed or purposive. Goal-oriented behavior can be stupid, clumsily devised and ineffective. In order to be thoroughly rational, a behavior or activity must be *teleologically efficacious,* effectively directed to the *telos* or end in view.

And finally, in order to be rational, the activity of creation cannot be thoroughly arbitrary. Creation cannot be, as some Hindu theology has it, the arbitrary, free play of the deity. In order to be rational, or reasonable, the activity of divine creation must be in some way *expressive* of God's character and nature. There must be some deep consonance, or harmony, between the nature of the act of creation and the character of the creator. For example, if God's purpose in creating is to share the value and joys of existence, and he is a perfect being, we would not expect creation to be in any way miserly or stingy. Instead, we would expect it to be liberal, magnanimous, profuse. Likewise, mirroring his perfection, we might expect a certain kind of efficiency in creation. Now, in one standard form of its usage, the word 'efficient' connotes the careful husbanding of limited resources. But God, of course, is not limited in resources. There is, however, another closely related sense of 'efficient,' according to which the efficient person just acts in such a way as to attain the greatest possible ratio of ends to means: the greatest possible results are brought about with only the most modest means imaginable. This form of efficiency clearly can be connected up with the property of being teleologically efficacious.

When we consider our universe, we obviously find a vast profusion of being. There is not just a single form of existence. There is not just a single star system or a single galaxy. There is rather a bewildering, awe-inspiring quantity and variety of beings to be found in the universe. Moreover, this profusion of being seems to be the result of very few basic laws, perhaps only one. It would be difficult to imagine greater efficiency in this proportioning of means to ends. And this is clearly a universe conducive to life. Within the extraordinarily broad spectrum of apparently possible universes, only a tightly delineated range would be hospitable to the rise of life, sentient existence, and conscious, intelligent beings capable of entering into moral and spiritual relations with each other and with a divine creator. From this perspective, our universe can appear purposive in just the way to be expected if it is in fact a created realm. In short, our universe can reasonably be thought to resonate with just those qualities it would be expected to have if it is indeed the product of a divine act of creation properly described as rational.

In the Judeo-Christian tradition of reflection on matters theological, divine creation is also typically believed to be free. At the most basic level, this means that the act of creation is not causally compelled or constrained by the action of anything existing independent of God. God did not just form our current cosmos out of partially resistant, or even perfectly malleable, previously existent material. No such mere forming or designing would capture the absoluteness of origination meant to characterize the fundamental act of divine creation. Traditionally, theologians and philosophers have sought to make this point by insisting that God has created this world *ex nihilo*, "from nothing." There is nothing distinct from God that has been used by God as raw material for the formation of this world. Nor is the created realm cut from the cloth of the divine being. It is produced strictly *ex nihilo*. If it were not, the act of production would not be free from the compulsion or constraint of previously existent being, nor would it be as great and dramatic an act as it is. God is not just a molder. He is an absolute maker. The freedom of his creative activity extends to this great an extremity.

Throughout the centuries, it has often been seen as central to the Christian conception of creation to affirm two other propositions about the scope of God's freedom with respect to the activity and products of creation:[5]

(1) God was free to refrain from creating any universe at all.
(2) In choosing to create, God was free to create some other universe instead of our universe.

However, distinct beliefs about the goodness and rationality of both the creator and his act of creation have been thought by some philosophers to create philosophical problems for each of these affirmations.

First of all, was God in fact free to refrain from bringing into existence any created beings at all? Could God have chosen to exist eternally without any creatures? Or was there some necessity about his creating something rather than nothing? As we shall see in the next section, an ontology, or theory of existence, can be developed according to which there are necessarily existing objects distinct from God that lack his aseity, such items as numbers, properties, and propositions, abstract objects that are necessarily created by a divine intellective activity. If there are such objects that depend on God for their necessary existence, he could not have refrained from creating them. His creation of them is necessary. But what about the creation of a universe of concrete individuals, of stars, planets, molecules and persons? Was God free to refrain from ever bringing into existence any such created realm as this? Was God free to refrain from creating any contingent objects, any objects which are individually such that any of them could have failed to exist? Some philosophers have thought not.

In the Middle Ages, a number of principles connecting being and goodness were widely endorsed by philosophically inclined theists. One of these we can refer to as the *principle of diffusiveness*:[6]

(PD) Goodness is essentially diffusive of itself and of being.

What this means is, roughly, that it is of the essence of goodness to be shared, communicated or conveyed. Goodness does not remain bottled up; it expresses itself. It is diffusive of itself and it is diffusive of being. Goodness is neither inert nor destructive. It is creative and productive of existent manifestations of itself. The principle of diffusiveness claims that goodness naturally expresses itself by bringing things into existence, by thus sharing the wondrous status of being.

If this principle is true, if goodness is essentially diffusive of itself and of being, then, some philosophers have thought, God was bound to create some contingent universe or other. For God is perfectly good and perfectly powerful.

He will thus seek to express his character by bringing things into existence, and nothing will prevent this manifestation of his goodness. He therefore *necessarily* will create contingent beings of some sort or other. And if this is true, he is not free not to create a contingent realm.

What is the status of the principle of diffusiveness? It seems to have been an influential part of Neo-Platonist metaphysics, which has been found attractive by some Christian thinkers. And it is natural to think of goodness as being, of its very essence, expressive of itself. It would be exceedingly odd to think of an individual as good, whose purported goodness was never expressed in any way at all. But is it necessary for perfect goodness to be manifested by the creation of contingent beings? It is hard to see how this interpretation of the principle could be thought compelling, or even very plausible, as it stands.

The moral goodness of a being is naturally expressed by what that being does. And many of the morally good things done by a person can be thought of as ways of passing along or sharing ("communicating," "diffusing") the resources of his goodness. It may even be the case that an individual's goodness would be somehow truncated or incomplete unless he had some other person with whom to commune and to share. But, as we shall see in the next chapter, Christians believe that God exists as three persons in one nature, eternally and necessarily. The eternally existing relations among these members of the divine *Trinity* are thought to encompass precisely the sort of communications of love and sharings of goodness that the legitimate insight behind the principle of diffusiveness requires. So in order for divine goodness to be expressed in an interpersonal way, it was not after all necessary for God to bring about the existence of a contingent universe containing created persons. It is expressed quite naturally in intratrinitarian relations.

But some philosophers seem to have thought that such an internal expression of divine goodness, internal to the divine Trinity, would not alone suffice to satisfy the full requirements of diffusiveness. Completeness would demand an expression of divine goodness outside the bounds of divine life. The first sort of expression of divine goodness possible outside the orb of deity would have to involve the creation of other entities. Thus, if there is to be external as well as internal manifestation of divine goodness, there must be divine creation.

It could be argued that if God necessarily creates numbers, properties and propositions, and exists as a divine Trinity, any reasonable completeness requirement concerning the diffusiveness of goodness is satisfied. God's goodness is expressed internally by trinitarian relations and externally by the giving of being to these necessary abstract entities. It is expressed both personally and metaphysically.

It seems that the only way a diffusiveness theorist could plausibly insist upon the necessity of God's creating some contingent universe or other would be by insisting upon the truth of some sort of *principle of plenitude* as well:

(PP) Perfect Goodness necessarily expresses itself in as many ways as are possible, and produces as many kinds of good as it can.

The existence of human beings is a good thing. It is possible for human beings to exist. Therefore, by (PP), God must create human beings. (PP) thus seems to entail the necessity not only of God's creating some contingent world or other, but much more specific results as well. In fact, it clearly entails too much.

It is possible for perfect goodness to express itself by providing me with many millions of dollars with which to do good, and perhaps buy a Jaguar sedan and a beach house. By (PP), I can be assured that God, being all-powerful as well as perfectly good, will diffuse his goodness in every way possible. Therefore, at some point, the check will be in the mail.

This, of course, is crazy. Yet (PP) is not an altogether crazy principle. Like (PD) it attempts to capture in logically precise form an insight about goodness. (PP) is an attempt to present, as a morally precise, metaphysical principle, the liberality or generosity that characterizes true goodness. The problem is that it is exceedingly difficult to capture the essence of love or goodness in this sort of metaphysically exact form.

It is natural for a man and a woman who love each other, and who are good people, to want to bring into existence a child, or children, with whom to share that love and toward whom to express that goodness. But it is not necessary for marital love and moral goodness to be expressed in this way. A person is not necessarily any less loving or good for choosing to remain celibate. A person physically or biologically prevented from having children of his or her own is not necessarily thereby condemned to an incomplete state of personal goodness. Bringing new life into existence is a natural expression of love and goodness. But it is not essential.

There is also no good reason to believe that maximization principles like (PP) actually succeed in requiring determinate tasks of an omnipotent being. First, there may be kinds of good, or forms of expression for goodness, that are noncompossible. So (PP) would have to be qualified accordingly. But even then, there is hardly any more reason to believe that there is a complete array, or a best complete array, of compossible forms of creatable good, or expressions of goodness, than there is to believe that there is any such thing as a highest possible number. And without this, the requirement of (PP), even suitably qualified, would be wholly indeterminate. But a wholly indeterminate principle cannot be taken to be an accurate articulation of any truth about reality. A wholly indeterminate principle is a principle that does not succeed in specifying precisely anything in particular about reality, despite any appearances to the contrary. And whenever nothing in particular is successfully specified with any precision about reality, no truth is accurately conveyed. In particular, it cannot be true that "Perfect Goodness necessarily expresses itself in as many ways as are possible, and produces as many kinds of good as it can" if there are no determinate, definite upper limits to the number of ways in which the expression of goodness is possible, or to the number of kinds of good that can be produced by the only sort of being who, in a theistic world-view, can be considered perfectly good, namely, the God who is also perfectly powerful. So it is reasonable to reject (PP), and thus the interpretation of (PD) that it provides. There is no compelling reason to follow those who believe that God must have created some contingent universe or other.

With this conclusion we have secured our right to conceive of the scope of divine freedom with respect to the act of creation to be so extensive as to encompass the freedom to refrain from bringing into being any contingent creatures such as ourselves at all. And such a conception is clearly consonant with the overall thrust of perfect being theology, when it is brought to bear on this topic. For it surely would seem greater for God to have the most extensive range of freedom we can imagine, consistent with his never acting in such a way as to violate his character or nature. And in addition, with the conception of God as free never to have created any contingent beings, we have secured the basis for another important insistence of Christian theologians that the very existence of a universe at all should be experienced and accepted by us as a free gift from God.

There is, however, one remaining objection to the claim that God was free not to create a contingent world. It typically proceeds by way of an objection to the other proposition about divine freedom mentioned when we began our examination of the freedom of creation:

(2) In choosing to create, God was free to create some other universe instead of our universe.

Critics of this claim have typically maintained that, as a perfect being, God's creative products must be perfect as well, since effects resemble their causes, or creations manifest the skill and greatness of their creators. So, as the greatest possible being, God could create only the best possible world. He has created this world. Therefore, this must be the best possible world, despite any appearances to the contrary. But if our universe is the best possible universe, God was not free to create some other universe instead. Proposition (2) is thus false.

The great philosopher Leibniz (1646-1716) reasoned in this way, saying:
Now this supreme wisdom, united to a goodness that is no less infinite, cannot but have chosen the best. For as a lesser evil is a kind of good, even so a lesser good is a kind of evil if it stands in the way of a greater good; and there would be something to correct in the actions of God if it were possible to do better.[7]
He further elaborates:
Now God cannot will to do anything other than that which he does, because, of necessity, he must will whatever is fitting. Hence it follows that all that which he does not, is not fitting, that he cannot will to do it, and consequently that he cannot do it.[8]
Leibniz even makes bold to describe how God chooses what to create. First, God knows all possibilities concerning what might exist. But then:
The wisdom of God, not content with embracing all the possibles,

penetrates them, compares them, weighs them one against the other, to estimate their degrees of perfection or imperfection, the strong and the weak, the good and the evil. It goes even beyond the finite combinations, it makes of them an infinity of infinities, that is to say, an infinity of possible sequences of the universe, each of which contains an infinity of creatures. By this means the divine Wisdom distributes all the possibles it had already contemplated separately, into so many universal systems which it further compares the one with the other. The result of all these comparisons and deliberations is the choice of the best from among all these possible systems, which wisdom makes in order to satisfy goodness completely; and such is precisely the plan of the universe as it is.[9]

And, making it all the more impressive, God accomplishes all this, according to Leibniz, atemporally.

This is clearly a majestic conception of the nature of the divine activity in creating. It has an undeniable, initial attractiveness for anyone committed to the method of perfect being theology. But its troubling result is to turn creation into something akin to a mechanical procedure. God does an immensely complex calculation, the result tells him what world to create, and from that result he *cannot* deviate. He was not free to create any world different from this world in even the smallest respect—one more atom, or one less elementary particle. And, of course, by the same reasoning, he was not free to refrain altogether from creating a world. It was necessary that he create the best.

Critics of Leibniz have been quick to point out that this world certainly does not look like the best possible world. It is easy to think of many ways in which things could be improved. There are evils that could be eliminated. There are goods that could be increased. Leibniz's response is to argue that "the evil that occurs is an inevitable result of the best."[10] From where we stand, it might seem as though the universe could be improved in a great many ways. We, however, fail to see the big picture. We are not in, and could not possibly be in, the best position to see how the many aspects of this world fit together into a whole and affect its overall value. Only God could occupy such a position. So appearances can be misleading and should not alone cause us to reject the result of this reasoning. Such is the reply available to Leibnizians.

In a highly influential article entitled "Must God Create the Best?" Robert M. Adams has resisted the Leibnizian view in a different way.[11] Adams suggests that God could create a less than best possible world without wronging anyone and without treating anyone, all things considered, unkindly. He maintains that God has no obligation to anyone to create only the best, and so God is free to graciously create good worlds which fall far short of being the best possible. But suppose Adams is right about God's having no such obligation. Do we expect manifestations of great goodness to be restricted to contexts of obligation to some particular person or other? Could the mere fact that no one need necessarily be wronged by an inferior creation suffice to justify God's creating less than the best? Adams does not rule out there being principles governing perfect goodness, truths constitutive of perfection, which would still generate Leibniz's conclusion.

But is it at all plausible to think that, among all the possibilities for creation, there is a single best possible world? Leibniz thought that if there were no such world, God would not have created at all. But refraining from creating would have resulted in the circumstance of there existing nothing but God alone, a circumstance or state of affairs with great value, but, as we have seen earlier in this chapter, a state of affairs with less overall value than that of God's existing along with a created universe. Leibniz, however, seems to have thought that God would never, and indeed could never, act without a fully sufficient reason for every aspect of his action. If there were no best possible world, and refraining from creation would not itself be a mode of divine action, God would have no sufficient reason to create any possible world, and so would refrain from creating anything, thereby refraining, in this regard, from acting.

The first point that must be made here is that we often think of ourselves as refraining from action in a certain regard only on account of reasons we have for so refraining. But if refraining from creating falls within the scope of possible reason giving, or the having of reasons, it is hard to see how Leibniz's argument here can go through, from his own point of view. God would have no sufficient reason to satisfy himself with the state of affairs of his existing bereft of any contingent creatures.

But there is a deeper problem with Leibniz's argument on this point. If God is truly free, it can be argued that he *can* act without a completely sufficient reason for every aspect of his action. This is just what the fullest possible range of freedom involves. This point blocks Leibniz's reasoning here and also counts against another, related Leibnizian conviction that if there were a class of best possible worlds, each surpassed by no other world but all tied in maximal value, then again God could not create at all, since he would have no sufficient reason to select one of those maximal worlds over the others. If he were truly free, however, he could just pick one.

From the perspective of a robust conception of the range of God's freedom, it thus does not seem to be the case that in order for God to create at all, there must be a single best possible universe he could bring into existence. And this is surely a good thing, since it is extremely difficult to suppose that there is a single scale of value on which all possible creations could be ranked, with one and only one surpassing all others with respect to degree of overall value. There are all sorts of values which different sorts of creatures might exemplify. And there is no good reason to believe that all these creaturely values are commensurable, comparable on the same scale of measurement. Some world A might be better than a rival world B in some respects, but with B surpassing A in some others, and the relevant values not such that they could be summed over and compared overall. There is no reason to suppose that things are as tidy as the Leibnizian perspective requires.

Furthermore, as many philosophers have pointed out over the centuries, for any world composed of a certain number of good creatures, or exemplifying a certain number of goods, n, there is always conceivable a greater world with $n + 1$ goods, or good creatures. So, on the simplest, barest grounds of additive value alone, it seems impossible to suppose that there can be a single best possible world. And without this, Leibniz's overall argument, of course, collapses.

If creation is to be good and rational, it must be consonant with the moral character of God. But if we are to think of it as truly free, we should be very wary of metaphysical principles whose effect would be to straitjacket the activity of God in this regard. If we have no good reason to think that there is or could be any such thing as a single best possible world creatable by God, and we have no good reason to suppose that there must be a sufficient reason for every single aspect of God's activity, then we have no good reason to follow Leibniz in believing that only a single world falls within the range of God's freedom to create. We can thus endorse both of the traditional affirmations that God was free to refrain from creating and free to create something other than what he did choose to create.

In rejecting Leibniz's conclusions, however, we do not have to reject all his insights. Surely it is fair to expect excellence of workmanship in any divine creation. Even if the perfection of the creator cannot be manifest in a single perfect creation alone, God's surpassing greatness will surely manifest itself in his creating only worlds of tremendous value. It is even natural to suppose that, with respect to whatever aspects of creation can be maximized, say, in certain kinds of efficiency, any world God creates will be the best possible in those respects. But this is far from supposing that there is a single best possible creation which alone God can bring into being. God will express himself in his activity. But his freedom of expression is vast.

Creaturely Dependence
We have been exploring the idea of God as a free, rational and good creator. In this section we shall examine a bit more the way in which all things thus depend upon God for their existence. All things distinct from God stand in a dependence relation to God, a relation that is both *direct* and *absolute*.

It is never the case that some created object *x* depends upon God only in the sense of depending for its existence upon some other created objects *y* and *z*, which in turn directly depend upon God. Every created object depends upon God directly for its existence. There is no indirectness about any such dependence relation. It is not just that my body depends on air and water and other physical substances for its existence, and these in turn depend upon God. Metaphysical or ontological dependence upon God, dependence for *being*, is, rather, in every case direct.

Such dependence is also absolute. God does not just launch things into existence and allow them subsequently to persist on their own. He does not just support an object's existence in only some of the circumstances in which it does exist. The dependence is thorough and continuous. To convey this idea many philosophers and theologians have spoken of God's activities of *creation and conservation* with respect to the world. God does not just bring things into existence and then take a hands-off approach to them. This is the error known as *deism*. God continually supports things in existence, moment to moment, throughout the entirety of their careers on the stage of reality. Divine conservation is thought to be so absolute a requirement for existence that, if God were to withdraw his support for our contingent universe for even an instant, it would all cease to be. To stress the importance of the divine activity to the continuous existence of any created object, some theologians have spoken of *continuous creation*. The idea is, roughly, that just as God creates an object at its first moment of existence, he re-creates it at all subsequent moments at which it exists. Yet, as the term 'continuous' indicates, this is not to be thought of as involving a staccato repetition of numerous, discrete creative acts. There is a continuity to the activity of divine creation that can be conceptualized either as conservation or as continuous creation. The important point is that at each instant of the existence of any created thing, it stands in a relation to God of absolute dependence.

There is another feature of absoluteness manifested by the most exalted version of a metaphysical doctrine of creation. Absolutely everything distinct from God depends on God for its existence. This is a foundational claim for any thoroughly theistic ontology. If God is the greatest possible being, a maximally perfect source of existence, then he is not just one more item in the inventory of reality. He is the hub of the wheel, the center and focus, the ultimate support, of all. The difference between theism and atheism is thus not just a disagreement over whether one entity of a certain description exists or not. It is a disagreement over the origin, and thus the ultimate nature, of everything.

God is often said to be *omnipresent*, or to have the property of *omnipresence*. He is present everywhere in the realm of his contingent creation. But his presence is not best understood as something akin to physical location. It is rather to be thought of as a function of his knowledge and power. God is thought to be present everywhere in the sense that his perfect knowledge and power extend over all. There is nothing outside the scope of his awareness or independent of the exercise of his creative power. He can act anywhere, and interact with anyone at any place. That is because he is ever-active and ever-aware at every place. All contingent physical objects, all contingent nonphysical objects, and all external relations that hold between and among them depend on God's activity of creation. Absolutely nothing in the realm of contingency exists independent of him.

But what of the realm of necessity? Are there necessarily existent entities distinct from God, such as properties and propositions or numbers, as was suggested in chapter six? And if so, how do they relate to God? Following Plato, many philosophers over the centuries have believed that there are such abstract objects, that they do necessarily exist, and that it follows from this that they exist independently of any exercise of divine power.

It is difficult, though, to conceive of what the existence of such independent objects might amount to. For, following Plato, abstract objects are not thought of as existing anywhere in the physical universe. They are instantiated, or exemplified, are true or false, or obtain, within the space-time realm. But they themselves have a more ethereal existence. Various human beings, for example, may be more or less just in their dealings with others. But justice itself, the property, the abstract entity, does not dwell in the land in any other than a metaphorical sense.

Abstract objects existing in their own realm of being are also typically thought of as standing outside any causal relations whatsoever. But then the existence of such things does look *sui generis*, different from anything else imaginable, and very strange. For what is the difference between a thing's existing and its not existing? In all clear and relatively uncontroversial cases of existence, it seems that for a thing to exist is just for it to have a place in a causal nexus, and thus to be capable of interacting with other existing things. If a tree exists outside my door, there is something out there I can bump into. There is something there that can cool me with its shade. Now, clearly, there are many things we cannot just bump into, but their existence causally impinges upon us in other ways. For example, there are things whose existence is manifest only due to their abilities to causally affect sensitive detection devices. But to say that something exists utterly outside any causal context at all is to break away from our clearest paradigms of what existence amounts to and to do so in a most decisive way.

Because of these and other worries, some philosophers have just denied that there is any robust sense in which abstract objects really exist at all. And if the position of these anti-Platonists is true, if there really are no necessary, abstract objects existing distinct from God, then from God's being the creator of all contingent things alone it would follow that there is nothing distinct from God which exists independent of him. But it is difficult to construct a satisfactory world-view without acknowledging some objective reality for numbers, properties, propositions and the like. So a great number of theistic philosophers have found the severe anti-Platonist move unacceptable. They have wanted to endorse the reality of numbers, properties, and propositions, and have seen a way of avoiding the problems which attend the conception of these entities as abstract objects existing autonomously, wholly independently in their own realm of reality. To this end they have taken up and developed St. Augustine's suggestion that these things be thought of as ideas in the mind of God. The *divine ideas tradition,* as this way of thinking is referred to, maintains that it is an ontologically efficacious divine intellective activity which is responsible for the existence of these things which we customarily classify as abstract objects. They are ideas which God thinks, eternally and necessarily. And the creative efficacy of his thought gives them being. They are caused to exist by being thought. And they are as they are in virtue of being thought of, or conceived, as they are by God.

This is a powerful metaphysical perspective: God is the creator not only of contingent reality, but also of all those necessities which comprise the modal framework of reality. All possible worlds exist in God as thoughts in the infinite divine mind. He is the creator of possibilities, the eternal upholder of necessities. God necessarily gives being to the realm of abstracta, *the framework of creation*—so called because all the possibilities and necessities resident in the divine mind structure all the available avenues of creative production, and thus all the ways the world can be.

It is not that God brings such things into existence at a time prior to which they have not existed. If they are eternal objects, he must eternally have been creating them. If they are necessities, he creates them, or gives them being, in every possible situation. But if they owe their being to God, as they must on an absolutely thoroughgoing theism, their necessity does not entail their aseity or ontological independence. Necessity is compatible with createdness. Only God is both necessary and independent.

If properties, propositions, and the like depend on God for their existence, they can be thought of as standing in a causal nexus—they are caused to be by God. And the realm of their existence is clarified—it is God's mind. So the troublesome worries of standard Platonism are avoided, but without the cost incurred by strict anti-Platonism. And, at the same time, we have a view which is clearly consonant with a thoroughly theistic ontology. All things, including these things, depend on God.

The theoretical benefits of such a view are great. When we admit that God cannot do the logically impossible, we are freed from having to think of God's activity being restricted by principles which have objective reality and force completely independent of him. The principles which structure his activities are ideas or thoughts in his mind whose existence derives from him. Likewise, when we say that God necessarily acts in accordance with moral principles, we do not have to think of objective moral laws as somehow existing "out there," independent of God, constraining his activity from above. They also are thoughts in the divine mind, existing as entertained by God, true as affirmed by him, necessary as endorsed by him in all possible worlds.

The creation of necessarily existent abstract objects by God is interestingly different from his creation of a contingent universe in many ways, and this should not be overlooked. The activity responsible for this realm will not be characterizable as "free, rational and good" in precisely all the same senses as the divine activity productive of a contingent world. It will be free only in the sense of being uncompelled and unconstrained by anything independent of God. Its rationality will be essential and of the most fundamental sort possible. Its goodness will consist precisely in giving rise to being which in turn gives rise to all the possibilities for contingent good. With necessities, there is no selection. There are no alternatives. But there can still be a dependence on God, a dependence which is both direct and absolute.

This is a fairly esoteric realm of divine creation, but it was important to consider, however briefly, because it is important to see how the theist can subsume all things distinct from God under the umbrella of divine creation. The greatest possible being will be the most thorough source of reality imaginable. Everything will testify to his greatness. Nothing will escape his domain, not even abstract objects.[12]

9

God Incarnate
and Triune

*A*lthough our intent in this book has been to explore the Christian conception of God, until now we have been examining primarily claims about God that are shared in common by many Christians, Jews and Muslims, as well as by philosophical theists who might hesitate to identify themselves with any historical religious tradition. In this chapter we shall turn our attention to some claims about God made by Christians alone. In particular, we shall focus in on two theological doctrines that together define what is distinctive about the Christian idea of God: the doctrine of the Incarnation and the doctrine of the Trinity.

The Doctrine of the Incarnation

By any reasonable account, the short life and ministry of Jesus of Nazareth had an extremely powerful impact on the people around him. Because of their experience of his life and teaching, and especially of the extraordinary events surrounding the end of his earthly career, his followers came to believe that creaturely categories were inadequate for conceptualizing who he is. Thus was born the distinctively Christian conviction that Jesus was, and is, both divine and human, God and man. The doctrine of the Incarnation is just the claim that in the case of Jesus the Christ, we are confronted by one person with two natures, human nature and the divine nature.

So the uniquely Christian proclamation was that Jesus is God Incarnate. Yet, he himself prayed to God and told his followers that when he left the earthly stage another comforter would come. This led to a threefold experience of divinity on the part of Christians, and a firm conviction that there is multiplicity within the unity of deity. It was this conviction that gave rise to the theologically precise doctrine of the Trinity, the belief that within the unity of the divine nature, God exists as three persons: God the Father, God the Son and God the Holy Spirit. With this development in the distinctively Christian view of deity, it was then possible to state the doctrine of the Incarnation with more precision. The claim is specifically that a properly divine person, God the Son, the second person of the divine Trinity, has taken on a human nature for us and our salvation. Before the time of the Incarnation, this person existed from all eternity as fully divine. Then, in the days of Herod the king, he took upon himself a fully human form of existence, yet never therein ceasing to be that which he eternally was. The early Christian experience of Christ thus finally led the Council of Chalcedon to decree in the year 451 that:

Following therefore the holy Fathers, we confess one and the same our Lord Jesus Christ, and we all teach harmoniously [that he is] the same perfect in Godhead, the same perfect in manhood, truly God and truly man, the same of a reasonable soul and body; consubstantial with the Father in Godhead, and the same consubstantial with us in manhood, like us in all things except sin . . . one and the same Christ, Son, Lord, unique; acknowledged in two natures without confusion, without change, without division, without separation—the difference of the natures being by no means taken away because of the union, but rather the distinctive character of each nature being preserved, and (each) combining in one person . . . not divided or separated into two persons, but one and the same Son and only-begotten God, Word, Lord Jesus Christ; as the prophets of old and the Lord Jesus Christ himself taught us about him, and the symbol of the Fathers has handed down to us.[1]

By so speaking, the Council presented the Christian church with the definition of orthodoxy on the ontology of Christ.

But, of course, the central philosophical problem which quickly arises here is not difficult to discern. In the Judeo-Christian vision of reality, no beings could be more different from each other than God, the creator of all, and any kind of creature. And even granting the doctrine that human beings are created in the image of God, humanity and divinity can certainly seem to be so different as to render it metaphysically and even logically impossible for any single individual to be both human and divine, *truly* God and *truly* man. As we have seen, God is omnipotent, omniscient, omnipresent, eternal, ontologically independent, and absolutely perfect. We human beings, of course, have none of these properties. And this surely seems to be no accident. Could I possibly have been a greatest possible being? Could you have been uncreated, eternally existent, and omnipresent in all of creation? Surely the logical complements, or opposites, of these divine properties are essential to you and to me. We could not exist without certain sorts of metaphysical limitations and dependencies—limitations and dependencies which are necessarily alien to the divine form of existence as it is conceived in Jewish and Christian theology. From this, critics of Chalcedon have concluded that there are properties necessary for being divine that no human being could possibly have, and properties essential for being human that no divine being could possibly have. The dramatic story told by Chalcedon is then viewed as a metaphysical impossibility.

The tension inherent in the two-natures doctrine of Christ was felt from the very earliest days of reflective Christian theology, and led to the existence of many conflicting opinions about Christ. The psilanthropists denied that Jesus was truly divine. The docetists concluded that he was not really human. The Arians denied that he was literally either. Apollinarians tried to whittle down the humanity to make room for the divinity. And Nestorians speculated on a composite Christ, one individual human person and one individual divine person, distinct from one another but acting in the closest possible relation of moral harmony. The church at large rejected all these strategies of partial or complete capitulation and insisted again and again on the Chalcedonian formula one person, two natures—truly God and truly man.[2]

The philosophical question here is whether orthodoxy embraces a possibility. Can the doctrine even possibly be true? In recent years many critics of the doctrine have claimed that it is clearly incoherent. But I believe that a strategy of defense is available which, surprisingly, is fairly simple.[3] The initial operative assumption is that, in trying to understand the doctrine, we should indeed begin with the most exalted conception of divinity, a down-to-earth conception of humanity, and the metaphysical constraints passed on to us by the early ecumenical councils of the church. Given these starting points, the procedure is then to turn back the philosophical arguments against the Incarnation's possibility by the use of conceptual distinctions and metaphysical postulations that flout no strong, reflectively held intuitions, and that together succeed in providing a picture of the metaphysics of God Incarnate that will accord with the portrayal of Christ in the documents of the New Testament.

In our attempt to understand and defend the doctrine of the Incarnation, we shall continue to use the most exalted conception of deity possible, that conception captured by perfect being theology. That is to say, we shall begin by thinking of any divine being as a greatest possible, or maximally perfect being. Divinity, or deity, we shall continue to construe as analogous to a natural kind, and thus as comprising a kind-essence, a cluster of properties individually necessary and jointly sufficient for belonging to the kind, or in this case, for being divine. We shall thus continue to think of omnipotence and omniscience, for example, as properties essential to deity. And, following the standard Anselmian intuitions we have discussed earlier, we shall take the strongly modalized properties of *necessary* omnipotence (omnipotence in all possible worlds, and at all times in any such worlds) and *necessary* omniscience to be ingredient in deity as well. Thus, on this picture, recall, no individual could possibly be God without being omnipotent. And no being could count as literally divine without having that attribute necessarily. The picture of God we are assuming thus holds that such properties as omnipotence, omniscience, omnipresence, eternality, moral perfection and ontological independence must belong to any individual who is divine, and must be had with the strongest possible modal status. If such an exalted conception of divinity can be squared with the doctrine of the Incarnation, then presumably more modest conceptions could be as well.

All other things being equal, it would seem that the more extreme a conception we have of deity, the more trouble we are going to have mapping out a coherent account of a divine Incarnation. But I do not think critics of the Incarnation usually go wrong by having too exalted a conception of divinity. Rather, I think they most commonly come to judge the Incarnation an impossibility mainly on account of an incorrect, metaphysically flawed conception of humanity. Only if we assume that it is necessary for being human, or for having a human nature, that an individual lack *any* of those properties ingredient in deity, do we have an obvious logical and metaphysical obstacle to the orthodox two-natures view of Christ. And I believe that the critics of the doctrine have come to hold such a conception of human nature only by missing some fairly simple distinctions and by ignoring some intriguing metaphysical possibilities.

First, there is the fairly well-known distinction between an *individual-essence*, and a *kind-essence*. An *individual-essence* is a cluster of properties essential for an individual's being the particular entity it is, properties without which it would not exist. A *kind-essence* is that cluster of properties without which, as we have seen, an individual would not belong to the particular natural kind it distinctively exemplifies. Of necessity, an individual can have no more than one individual-essence, or individual nature, but it does not follow from this, and is not, so far as I can tell, demonstrable from any other quarter, that an individual can have no more than one kind-essence. And this is surely a good thing, for if such an argument could be made out, it would block from the start the doctrine of the Incarnation, at least the orthodox two-natures view, without the need of turning to consider the specifics of divinity and humanity.

Once we have recognized a distinction like that between individual-essences and kind-essences, we can see that necessities intuitively thought to characterize individual human beings cannot automatically be deemed to be such in virtue of those beings' common human nature, as part of the kind-essence of humanity. You and I, and any of our neighbors, may be such that we necessarily are noneternal, created beings, and we may share that modal characterization with all of the human beings living on the surface of the earth today without its at all following that this necessity constitutes part of what it is to have a human nature. It may be the case that all of our individual essences incorporate these modal properties of limited metaphysical status without its being the case that these properties are metaphysical prerequisites for exemplifying the natural kind of being human. Of course, critics of the Incarnation have discerned such necessities while thinking about human beings, have identified them simply as ingredients in human nature, and, pointing out that quite contrary necessities form the divine nature, have gone on to conclude that it is impossible for a properly divine being to take on human nature.[4] But more caution is needed here than is customarily exercised. In drawing their conclusions about what is essential for being human, critics of the Incarnation have, I think, made some errors which can be highlighted and then avoided by the use of two more straightforward distinctions.

In trying to enumerate the properties essential for being human, some theologians have included the property of being sinful, but this is a property the decree of Chalcedon explicitly denies of Christ. Why would anyone ever think it is part of the kind-essence of humanity? Probably because they have employed a very simple and very inadequate method for determining the elements of human nature, a method that we can call the *look-around-town approach:* Look around town, and what do you see? Every human being you come across shares numerous properties with every other human in town, including, most likely, the property of being sinful. To conclude that being sinful is thus a part of human nature is, however, to miss a simple distinction. There are properties which happen to be *common* to members of a natural kind, and which may even be *universal* to all members of that kind, without being *essential* to membership in the kind. Mere observation alone can suffice to establish commonality. Thought experiments and modal intuitions must be drawn upon to determine necessity, or kind-essentiality. Once these distinctions are properly drawn, we can acknowledge the commonality of sinfulness among human beings while at the same time following Chalcedon in denying both its strict universality and its presence in the kind-essence which we call human nature.

Such properties as those of being contingent, created, noneternal, nonomnipotent, nonomniscient and nonomnipresent are certainly common to human beings. Apart from the case of Christ, they are even, presumably, universal human properties. But I submit that they are not kind-essential human properties. It is not true that an individual must be a contingent being, noneternal and nonomnipotent in order to exemplify human nature. It is possible for an individual to be human without being characterized by any of these limitation properties. And so it is possible for an individual who essentially lacks such properties, an individual who is properly divine, to take up at the same time a human nature.

The many properties of metaphysical limitation and dependence that characterize you and me do so, then, not because they are essential elements in our common human nature. They may characterize you and me necessarily. Presumably, they do. But it is not in virtue of our being human; rather, it is in virtue of our being the humans we are. Such properties may partially comprise our respective individual essences, or, more likely, may characterize us in virtue of the fact that we created human beings are *merely human*—we are no more than human. Humanity crowns our ontological status as the greatest foothold we have in the grand scheme of things. We are *fully human:* we have all the properties constituting the kind-essence of humanity. But we are merely human as well: we have certain limitation properties in virtue of being God's creatures. Those limitations need not be ingredient in our humanness, only in our creatureliness. Thus, God the Son, through whom all things are created, need not have taken on any of those limitation properties distinctive of our creatureliness in order to take on a human nature. He could have become fully human without being merely human.

Now, all these distinctions and defensive moves may be fine, each taken in itself, one by one. But the net result of applying them to a full defense of the Incarnation can appear problematic in the extreme. When we consult the pages of the New Testament, we see in the portrait of Jesus the workings of a mind which, extraordinarily wise and discerning as it may be, seems less than omniscient, and which appears, for all its strength, to lack the power of omnipotence in itself, having to turn heavenward for resources just as we do. We see a mind apparently conditioned by the first-century Palestinian world-view. We see a man who shared the anguish and joys of the human condition. Our metaphysical distinctions cannot be allowed to blind us to this. And it would be both foolish and heterodox to minimize it. We need a picture of the Incarnation that will account for all of these appearances.

Two Pictures of God Incarnate

We are completely clear on what it means to begin with an exalted conception of divinity. It may not be clear at all what I meant when I added above that we should also start with a down-to-earth conception of humanity. Now is the time to make it clear. Taking on a human nature involves taking on a human body and a human mind, no more and no less. What essentially constitutes a human body and a human mind we wait upon a perfected science, or a more complete revelation, to say. We have neither a very full-blown nor a very fine-grained understanding of either at this point. But we do know well enough what a human body is, and what a human mind is, for it to be informative to be told that taking on such a body and mind is taking on a human nature. It is both necessary and sufficient for being human. This is almost embarrassingly simple as metaphysics goes. No modal razzle-dazzle, no ontological arcana: If you have a human body and mind, you have a human nature—you exemplify the kind-essence of humanity. This is surely a down-to-earth conception of humanity if anything is.

For God the Son to become human, he thus had to take on a human body and a human mind, with all that entails. He did not have to become a created, contingent being. He just had to take on a created, contingent body and mind of the right sort. And so he was born of Mary the virgin and lived a human life.

But how did he manage this? Isn't it clear that taking on a human body and mind in order to live a human life involves taking on limitations of knowledge, power and presence? And aren't such limitations incompatible with divinity? As we have noted, the New Testament pictures an extraordinary individual living out a life among his fellows from limited human resources. How is this to be reconciled with his being divine? Some philosophers and theologians have believed that Jesus' limits force us to tone down a bit our conception of what deity consists in. They have come to think that facing up to what the New Testament shows us concerning Jesus' real limits requires us to conclude that in becoming incarnate he—that is, God the Son—gave up temporarily some of his unrestricted divine attributes, for example, his omniscience, his omnipotence and his omnipresence. This, they think, was required in order for him to take on the limitations involved in living a genuinely human life and sharing fully in our common human condition. This is the story told by *kenotic Christology* (from the Greek word *kenosis*, or "emptying"). If kenotic Christology is true, if God the Son temporarily empties himself, giving up his properly divine power, relinquishing his complete knowledge, and restricting his presence to the confines of his mortal shell while nonetheless remaining divine, it cannot be that divinity necessarily comprises or requires omnipotence, omniscience and omnipresence. For if during the early sojourn, the Second Person of the Trinity was divine but was without these exalted properties, they cannot be among those things required for true deity. As kenotic Christology is incompatible with seeing divinity as, at least in part, constituted by necessary omnipotence, necessary omniscience and necessary omnipresence, so it is also incompatible with holding all the simple, nonmodalized properties of omnipotence, omniscience and omnipresence to be requisites of divinity.

Well, then, on the kenotic view, what *are* the necessary truths about divinity? What is it to be God? The kenotic suggestion, perhaps, is something like this: In order to be literally divine, it is necessary for an individual to have in all possible worlds the property of *being omnipotent unless freely and temporarily choosing to be otherwise,* the property of *being omniscient unless freely and temporarily choosing to be otherwise,* and likewise for omnipresence. On this modally less extreme view of divinity, a divine being is not necessarily invulnerable to ignorance and weakness. He can render himself vulnerable to these deficiencies, he can take them on, while yet remaining truly divine.

Kenotic Christology began to be developed during the nineteenth century and continues to be refined today despite numerous critics—many of whom have just failed to grasp the subtlety with which the position can be deployed. And it must be said in behalf of the kenotic strategy that (1) what it seeks to accommodate in the biblical portrayal of Christ is indeed crucial to preserve, and (2) it is altogether legitimate and proper for a Christian to apply his convictions arising out of divine revelation and the events of salvation history to his philosophical theology, and in particular to his philosophical conception of God. There must be a dynamic interaction between what *a priori*, intuitive, or purely philosophical constraints there are on philosophical theology and the agreed data of revelation. The kenotic maneuver presents us with an intriguing possibility, yet I must admit that I have a hard time finding it satisfactory. It presents us with a far less exalted and less theoretically satisfying conception of Christ's deity. Its way of redefining the basic divine attributes seems extremely *ad hoc,* an exercise in metaphysical gerrymandering reflective of no more general philosophical distinctions. And my misgivings about such an account of Christ's deity are not without parallel in the weightiest theological treatises.

During the early years of the fifth century, Pope Leo wrote an essay on the Incarnation which the Council of Chalcedon embraced as properly capturing the two-natures view of Christ. Known as *The Tome of Leo,* it says of Christ that, among other things:

He took on him "the form of a servant" without the defilement of sins, augmenting what was human, not diminishing what was divine; because that "emptying of himself," whereby the Invisible made himself visible, and the Creator and Lord of all things willed to be one among mortals, was a stooping down of compassion, not a failure of power. Accordingly, the same who, remaining in the form of God, made man, was made Man in the form of a servant, so the form of a servant does not impair the form of God.[5]

A sophisticated kenotic Christology can be argued to preserve the letter of Leo's claims, but I have difficulty seeing how it can be thought to be true to the spirit of those claims. But in case this is unclear, consider the great theologian Athanasius (c. A.D. 293-373), who wrote earlier concerning the incarnate Christ:

He was not, as might be imagined, circumscribed in the body, nor, while present in the body, was he absent elsewhere; nor, while he moved the body, was the universe left void of his working and providence; but, thing most marvelous, Word as he was, so far from being contained by anything, he rather contained all things himself; and just as while present in the whole of creation, he is at once distinct in being from the universe, and present in all things by his own power, . . . thus, even while present in a human body and himself quickening it, he was, without inconsistency, quickening the universe as well.[6]

So, for Athanasius, it seems that Christ was not limited in power, knowledge and effect to the workings of his human mind and body during the time of the Incarnation. There is no restricting of his being to the confines of the human alone. This is surely no kenotic, metaphysical emptying or relinquishing of the properly divine status or functioning. While having a human body and mind and living out a human life on this terrestrial globe, Christ nonetheless retained all of the resources and prerogatives of divinity in the most robust sense.

But can we make sense of such a view? Can we indeed have it all, the fullness of humanity and the fullness of divinity? I think so, for there is an alternative to the kenotic picture of Christ, an alternative which has been called the *two-minds view*.[7] On this account of the Incarnation, taking on a human body and mind did not require or involve relinquishing the proper resources of divinity. Just as we saw that God the Son's taking on of a created, contingent body and mind does not entail that he himself was a created, contingent being, so, on the two-minds view, his taking on of a body and mind limited in knowledge, power and presence does not entail that he himself, in his deepest continuing mode of existence, was limited in knowledge, power or presence. Rather, in the case of God Incarnate we must recognize something like two distinct minds or systems of mentality. There is first what we can call the eternal mind of God the Son, with its distinctively divine consciousness, whatever that might be like, encompassing the full scope of omniscience, empowered by the resources of omnipotence, and present in power and knowledge throughout the entirety of creation. And in addition to this divine mind, there is the distinctly earthly mind with its consciousness that came into existence and developed with the conception, human birth and growth of Christ's earthly form of existence. The human mind drew its visual imagery from what the eyes of Jesus saw, and its concepts from the languages he learned. This earthly mind, with its range of consciousness and self-consciousness, was thoroughly human, Jewish and first-century Palestinian in nature. By living out his earthly life from only the resources of his human body and mind, he took on the form of our existence and shared in the plight of our condition.

So, on the two-minds view, the Incarnation involved not just a duality of abstract natures, but a duality of consciousness or mentality, which was introduced into the divine life of God the Son. The two minds of Christ should be thought of as standing in something like an asymmetric accessing relation: The human mind was contained by, but did not itself contain, the divine mind; or, to portray it from the other side, the divine mind contained, but was not contained by, the human mind. Everything present to the human mind of Christ was thereby present to the divine mind as well, but not vice versa. There was immediate, direct access from the human mind to the divine mind, but no such converse immediacy of access. Insofar as Christ normally chose to live his earthly life out of his human resources alone, the words he spoke and the actions he performed by means of the body were words and actions arising out of his human mind. He had all the mental, intellectual, emotional and volitional resources we all have, lacking none. And it was these, not his divine resources, that he typically drew on for the personal history he enacted on this earth. But this living of a human life through human resources was, on the two-minds view, going on at the same time that he, in his properly divine form of existence, was continuing to exercise his omnipotence, with the wisdom of his omniscience, in his omnipresent activities throughout creation.

Can we, however, really hope to understand the two-minds view? Can we attain any firm grasp of what it might have been like for God Incarnate to have at one and the same time a limited human consciousness and an overarching divine mind? To some extent, I think we can. There are numerous earthly phenomena with which we are familiar that can be taken to provide very helpful, partial analogies to the two-minds view of Christ. There seem to exist, for example, cases of dreams in which the dreamer both plays a role within the environs of the dream story, operating with a consciousness formed from within the dream, and yet at the same time, *as* dreamer, retains an overarching consciousness that the drama of the dream is just that—only a dream. Another sort of analogy can be provided by thought experiments dealing with artificial intelligence, in which two physical systems are each such as to be credited with mentality, and yet stand in such an asymmetric accessing relation that one can be considered a subsystem of the other, with its own distinctive origin and functions, but at the same time belonging to the unity of a larger system of mentality. And then there are numerous, powerful, partial analogies available in the literature dealing with human cases of multiple personality. In many such cases, there seem to be different centers or spheres of consciousness standing in an asymmetric accessing relation to an overarching or executive self, and ultimately belonging to one person. Of course, human cases of multiple personality involve severe dysfunction and undesirable traits starkly disanalogous to anything we want to acknowledge in the Incarnation. But this just helps us to see where the specific limits of this sort of analogy lie.

There are also certain phenomena having to do with hypnosis, brain commissurotomy, self-deception and *akrasia*, or weakness of will, in which there seem to be operative different levels or spheres of awareness, information retention and processing, or, in general, mentality which are, in important metaphysical ways, analogous to what the two-minds view recognizes in the case of the Incarnation. Again, it must be stressed that the negative aspects of these extraordinary, worldly cases of multiple mentality are not meant at all to characterize the Incarnation, and in fact can be argued decisively not to cloud Christ's case in the least. These are only partial analogies, which provide us with some imaginative grip on the two-minds picture.

One of the best analogies may be provided by the claim of twentieth-century psychologists that every normal human being partakes of a variety of levels of mentality. Consider for example the very simple distinction of the conscious human mind, the seat of occurrent awareness, from the unconscious mind. In most standard accounts of such a distinction, the unconscious mind stands to the conscious mind in much the same relation that the two-minds view sees between the divine and human minds in the case of Christ. God the Son, on this picture, took on every normal level or sphere of human mentality, but enjoyed the extra depth as well of his properly divine mindedness.

One interesting feature of all these analogies which have to do with human psychological phenomena is that they point toward what some theorists are calling a "multimind" view of persons in general.[8] On this sort of a view, a person is, or at least it is inevitable that a person potentially has, *a system of systems of mentality,* to use the broadest possible terminology. This systems view of the person is in close accord with the more generalized view of all of life as involving hierarchically stratified systems of organization and control, but is arrived at with evidence of its own, not as just the application of the more general view to the case of persons.

We can develop a systems view here in such a way that all finite mental systems are metaphysically open-ended for hierarchical subsumption by deeper, or higher, systems—use whichever vertical metaphor you prefer. Epistemolog-ically, we typically come to recognize the existence of a multiplicity of mental systems in the case of a human being only when things go awry, as in multiple personality, commissurotomy, or what is called self-deception. But the systems view is that what we thus come to recognize, the multiplicity of systems of mentality, is always there in some form in normal cases as well, although functioning very differently, and thus being manifested very differently, if at all, to normal observation.

It is, of course, not my claim that a systems view of mentality proves the two-minds view of Christ, that it serves as any evidence for the truth of this theological view, or even that it establishes the possibility of this picture of the Incarnation. It only provides us with a general account of mentality that is thoroughly consonant with the main features of the metaphysical postulations distinctive of the two-minds view, and thus gives us a vantage point from which to come to better understand the view. It also helps to answer some questions that can otherwise seem to yield troubling problems for the view.

Did Christ have erroneous beliefs, such as would have been acquired through the natural functioning of his human mind in the social and intellectual environment in which he lived? Did he have a geocentric picture of the cosmos? Did he really not know who touched the hem of his garment? He had a limited human mind and a divine mind, so what is the answer, yes or no? Our ordinary practices and locutions for belief ascription can lead to puzzling questions concerning God Incarnate. But I think the two-minds view, rather than creating such puzzlement, actually helps us to see through it. First of all, we must be cautious about assuming that our ordinary linguistic practices are completely in order here, in such a way that they can act as altogether reliable touchstones of truth. If it is asked exactly what Christ believed, the two-minds view will direct us to ask what information was contained in his earthly mind, and then what information was contained in his divine mind. And this sort of response is to be expected on any multimind view of the person, or on any multisystems approach to mentality. Our ordinary, simple ways of posing and answering such questions in mundane contexts may provide less than absolutely reliable guidance where such metaphysical precision is required, as in the doctrine of the Incarnation.

But if the question is pressed concerning what the person God the Son himself believed on this or that issue, evading the question by appealing to the duality of minds can appear to threaten the unity of the person, and thus the coherence of the whole picture. The response of dividing the question does remind us of something important. God the Son Incarnate had two minds and chose to live out the life of the body on this earth normally through the resources of the human mind alone. That was the primary font of most of his earthly behavior and speech. Nevertheless, if the question is really pressed, if it is insisted that we be prepared, in principle, to say what he, the individual person, believed about this or that, we must appeal to the feature of hierarchical organization endemic to a systems view of mentality and, recognizing the priority of the divine, represent God the Son's ultimate belief state as captured in his divine omniscience. This feature of hierarchical organization thus does not leave us in puzzlement concerning the final story about the person.

This move seems to indicate a compatibility between metaphysical double-mindedness and personal unity. But what exactly does the personal unity of Christ consist in on the two-minds view? What makes the human mind of Jesus a mind of God the Son? A critic of this account of the Incarnation could point out, for example, that on the standard view of God as utterly omniscient, any divine person stands in a direct, immediate and complete asymmetric accessing relation to the mind of every human being. If standing in this relation is what makes Jesus' earthly mind a mind of God, all our minds are minds of God, and thus we are all divine incarnations. If this were a safe inference from the two-minds view, I think it is safe to say it would serve as an effective refutation of the view, demonstrating its unacceptability.

The accessing relation alone, however, is not intended by the two-minds view to count as a sufficient condition of Incarnation. Information flow by itself does not constitute mental, metaphysical ownership. So, what does? I must admit that I am no more sure about how to spell out what constitutes metaphysical ownership in the case of the Incarnation than I am about how to spell out exactly what it is for a range of mentality to be a part of my own mind, or to belong to me. There are mysteries here in any case, not just in the case of what the two-minds view claims about the Incarnation. But, fortunately, this is not all there is to be said.

What we can refer to as my human mental system was intended by God to define a person. If my human mental system is subsumed or overridden by any other causal system, my personal freedom is abrogated. The complete human mental system of Jesus was not intended alone to define a person. It was created to belong to a person with a divine mind as well as the ultimate, hierarchically maximal mental system. At any point during the metaphysical event of the Incarnation, it is thus possible that the human capacities of Christ, or the entirety of what we are calling his human mental system, be subsumed and overridden by the divine mind, without its being the case that any person's freedom is thereby abrogated. And this is a crucial difference between Jesus and any other human being, indeed, between Jesus and any free-willed *creature* of God. When our attention has been directed to this, it has been directed to the distinctiveness of the metaphysics of God Incarnate.

We are always in danger of misunderstanding the doctrine of the Incarnation, and the two-minds view of Christ in particular, if we forget that here, as in other properly metaphysical contexts, 'person' is an ultimate, ontological status term, not a composition term. The entirety of the human mental system of God the Son did not serve to compose a human person distinct from the person who was and is properly divine, because having the status of exemplifying a human body-mind composite was not the deepest truth about the ontological status of that individual. The personhood of Jesus was a matter of his ultimate ontological status and nothing less. This is the claim of the Christian tradition.

The two-minds view of Christ is extraordinarily interesting, philosophically and theologically, and, at least *prima facie,* it seems to me strongly preferable to the alternative of kenotic Christology. Something like one or the other of these pictures of the Incarnation is necessary, I think, if we are to make full sense of the manifest earthly career of Jesus from the perspective of a commitment to his divinity; or, to put it the other way around, if we are to make full sense of a belief in his divinity from the perspective of the manifest, earthly career of Jesus. From either point of view, we need some such account of the metaphysics of God Incarnate.

The Doctrine of the Trinity
We already have indicated, in the briefest way possible, what the doctrine of the Trinity is. Now is the time to lay it out a bit more carefully. The threefold

Christian experience of God, as recorded in the New Testament, has led to the Christian understanding of God as existing in threefold form—three persons in the unity of one divine nature. Jesus, as we have seen, is believed to be divine, God Incarnate. But he himself often indicated that he saw himself as standing in relation to a distinct divine person. He seems often to have prayed to God and to have said of himself that he had been sent by his heavenly father. So Christians have come to recognize, at the level of deity, both God the Father and God the Son, who have also come to be known, respectively, as the First Person and the Second Person of the divine Trinity. The special Comforter, whom Jesus promised his followers after his departure and who was believed to have come upon the church at Pentecost, endowing those early Christians with supernatural gifts, drawing others to Christ and working sanctification in the lives of all true believers, is identified in Christian theology as the Third Person of the divine Trinity, God the Holy Spirit. So we have as the object of Christian faith and worship three divine persons. But Christians have insisted from the earliest days that this is in no important way like pagan polytheism; it is not the worship of three independent gods.[9]

In any attempt to understand the doctrine of the Incarnation, the challenge is to secure the unity of the person of Christ while at the same time acknowledging the real distinctness of his two natures. In understanding the doctrine of the Trinity, the challenge is to balance the distinctness of the persons with the real unity of the divine nature, a unity sufficient to justify the Christian insistence that monotheism has not been utterly abandoned, that, in the words of Deuteronomy, "The LORD our God is one God" (Deut 6:4). But how is this to be done?

Throughout the centuries, many theologians and philosophers have tried to explain both the threeness and the oneness of the Trinity, while staying within the boundaries for an acceptable account laid down by the early church. In reaction against the views of the popular theologian Arius, who had claimed that at the deepest level of his being Jesus the Christ was a created being, brought into existence by God the Father at a particular time, the Council of Nicaea (A.D. 325) declared:

We believe in one God, the Father almighty, maker of all things, visible and invisible;

And in one Lord Jesus Christ, the Son of God, only-begotten, that is, from the substance of the Father, God from God, light from light, true God from true God, begotten not made, of one substance with the Father, through whom all things came into being, things in heaven and things on earth, who because of us men and because of our salvation came down and became incarnate, becoming man, suffered and rose again on the third day, ascended to the heavens, and will come to judge the living and the dead; And in the Holy Spirit.

But as for those who say, there was when He was not and, before being born He was not, and that He came into existence out of nothing, or who assert that the Son of God is from a different hypostasis or substance, or is created, or is subject to alteration or change—these the Catholic church anathematizes.[10]

The fully divine status of the Holy Spirit, who is no more than mentioned here (since the controversy addressed was over the Son), was made clear at the Council of Constantinople a few years later in 381. As the trinitarian language came to be developed in the Western church, the Son was said to have been eternally "begotten" by the Father, whereas the Spirit eternally "proceeded" from the Father and the Son. So, although the three persons were regarded as equally divine, there was believed to be a hierarchy of dependence relations within the exalted realm of divinity.

All the attempts to spell out the doctrine of the Trinity can be thought of as located along a spectrum, at one end of which is the error of *modalism,* and at the other end of which is *polytheism.* The heresy of modalism is the claim that the three "persons" are merely three appearances of God, or three roles God plays in salvation history. It is a view which holds that really there is only one divine individual, one ultimate bearer of the properties of divinity beneath these three "masks" or "modes of appearance." And, of course, polytheism is the belief in two or more distinct and independent deities. Modalism and polytheism are the Scylla and Charybdis between which all orthodox accounts of the Trinity must steer.

Within this range, we can distinguish between *singularity theories of the Trinity,* which attempt to stress the unity of the divine nature, without falling into modalism, and *social theories of the Trinity,* which attempt to highlight the diversity or distinctness of the three persons, without falling into polytheism. A social theory represents the Trinity as a community of three distinct persons, each with a distinct center of consciousness and will, yet all existing with the others in as close a relation of harmony and love as it is possible to stand in.

In a recent essay, "Could There Be More Than One God?" Richard Swinburne develops a fascinating version of a social theory.[11] Swinburne calls our attention to the fact that one important aspect of perfect goodness is perfect love. Now love must have an object, but, even more importantly, love must be shared. For in self-love one's love has an object, but surely, in order to be a fully loving person, any individual must extend his or her love beyond the bounds of self alone. Divine love is not only complete, it is eternal and necessary. So there must exist on the part of God some sharing of love which is both eternal and necessary. As we saw in our discussion of creation in chapter eight, some philosophers and theologians have argued that, because of the requirements of perfect love, God must of necessity create some contingent being or other, or some world of contingent beings, with whom to share his love. Otherwise, his love would not be complete. But this conclusion runs counter to the firmly held traditional claim that God was free not to create any contingent things at all. Let us refer to this problem as the *problem of the lonely God.*

Swinburne offers a solution to the problem of the lonely God which blocks this argument and avoids the conclusion that God needed to create something contingent like you or me. Suppose, he begins, that there is a primordial divine being with such attributes as omnipotence, omniscience, necessity and perfect goodness. Suppose this being eternally and necessarily exemplifies all the attributes constitutive of deity. He could not exemplify them all, however, without sharing love in the deepest and most complete way possible. But the deepest and most complete way of sharing love would be to share of oneself in giving being to another from one's own being. This divine individual thus eternally and necessarily begets, from his own being, a distinct person who, as so begotten, is a true Son of the Father, divine from divine being. We thus have a conception of a primordial divine being's giving existence, eternally and necessarily, to a second divine person with whom love can be perfectly shared. But there is another element of love, or form of love, yet to be attended to.

Not only is it possible for one person to share love with a second person, it is possible for two people to join together in sharing mutual love with a third. Think of the way in which married couples naturally seek to express their love in the giving and nurturing of a distinct life. This seems to be a form of love, or a richness of love, distinct from the sharing which goes on only between one person and another. But the perfection of divine love must encompass every basic form, or level of richness, possible for love. So we must suppose that a third divine person proceeds from the Father and the Son, eternally and necessarily, as the object of the mutuality of their ultimate giving and sharing. This divine person, the Holy Spirit, both is loved by, and in turn loves, each of the other persons of the Trinity. And there is completeness in mutual love. The Father and Son love the Spirit. The Son and Spirit love the Father. The Father and Spirit love the Son. All the forms and depths of love are manifest within divinity, and there is no need of any other divine person to make possible the complete manifestation of love. On this view, there are necessarily three distinct persons within divinity, and just as necessarily, there are no others. Thus, there exists the divine Trinity worshiped by Christians.

Some philosophers have suggested that there could not possibly exist more than one omnipotent being, for if there were two or more, their wills could potentially conflict.[12] But there could not be any possible resolution of a conflict between omnipotent beings. So, these philosophers have thought, we must conclude that there cannot be more than one omnipotent individual. What exactly follows, however, is just that if there is more than one omnipotent being, they must be necessarily harmonious in will. But from where will that harmony come? What will be the principle of division of labor, or who will set the rules, so to speak, for the patterns of co-operation among equally omnipotent beings? Swinburne suggests that among omnipotent beings, there must be a hierarchy of responsibility or authority over such matters, and that this in itself indicates that there could not be a multiplicity of divine beings unless their ontology was much like what he argues to be the case in the Trinity. For Father, Son and Holy Spirit, the coordination responsibilities, or authority, will lie with the Father, as the primordial member of the Trinity. It would be a condition of the eternal and necessary existence of the other two persons that in some metaphysically prior way, the matters of coordination and harmonious function had already been settled. So they must eternally and necessarily derive from the Father. The New Testament itself contains reflections of this, as God the Son Incarnate seems clearly to defer to the Father and to the authority of the Father.[13]

On this view of the Trinity as consisting in a society of divine persons, we must therefore understand the possible exercise of the omnipotent power of each of the persons as constrained by the opportunities provided by whatever rules of coordination the Father lays down. Since such rules are necessary and come from a perfectly good person, Swinburne argues, each of the other members of the Trinity would necessarily welcome them and abide by them. And this is no unfortunate limitation on the freedom of each of the divine persons, as it is a necessary condition of the highest form of existence, encompassing the completeness of perfect goodness and love.

But a few final words of clarification are needed if we are to hope to attain a good grasp of this sort of social theory of the Trinity. The decree of Nicaea insisted that the Son was not made of previously existing created material, and that he was not created *ex nihilo* at some point in time, as presumably is the case with every contingent object. The *generation* of the Son and what has been called the *spiration* of the Spirit are viewed as sharings of the being or substance of God the Father, sufficient for the eternal and necessary coexistence of two divine persons distinct from the Father, himself a divine person. Each of them has all the attributes constitutive of deity. But it is obvious that our understanding of aseity, or ontological independence, must be qualified somewhat on this view. For the Son depends on the Father, and the Spirit depends on the Father and the Son. Only the Father's existence is primordial and underived. But as we have seen on this view, insofar as being perfectly good is a condition of his existence, and the existence of the Son and Spirit as objects and sharers in love is necessary for his goodness, he bears some sort of dependence relation to them. But neither the Trinity itself, nor any of the members of the Trinity, stands in any relation of ontological dependence on any source of being prior to, or independent of, either the Father or the community all three form. The divine Trinity itself is ontologically independent and thus self-sufficient.

On this view, each member of the Trinity can be viewed as a greatest possible being, such that no other being could possibly be greater. Or we could judge there to be an internal hierarchy of greatness within the Trinity, such that no being outside the Trinity can be as great as the Spirit or the Son, but God the Father is greater than all (as some readings of John 10:29 might be taken to suggest) in the interpretive context of trinitarian doctrine. But in order to avoid another heresy, that of *subordinationism*, this latter view would have to insist on the underlying divine unity, that each of the persons of the Trinity is indeed fully divine. Another distinct application of the Anselmian perspective could specify that it is the Trinity itself which is properly considered the greatest possible being. My point here is only that social trinitarians could make various moves at this point to square their theory with the perspective of perfect being theology.

To avoid polytheism of the sort rejected by the early church fathers, social trinitarians must insist on the unity of the divine essence (the persons all share the attributes of deity), the unity of the divine substance (they all share in the being of the Father), and the unity that exists on the level of divine activity: What one member of the Trinity performs, all are said to share in performing, each in his own way, so full and deep is their cooperation.

But social trinitarians are nonetheless often said to be polytheists, however strongly they protest and proclaim their monotheism. Many theologians and Christian philosophers are very uncomfortable with any social theory of the Trinity, and thus seek to develop instead some form of what I have called a singularity theory of God's tri-unity. The heresies associated with singularity theories involve holding that the threeness of God consists only in his manner of presentation of himself to us. Christian orthodoxy has insisted that the diversity of the divine be not just a matter of appearance, but a matter of eternal, ontological reality. Numerous biblical passages seem to suggest this (Jn 1:1-3; 8:58; 17:1-26), and the problem of the lonely God seems to demand it. But singularity theories have faced difficulties in attempting an account of the Trinity adequate for accommodating those New Testament passages and avoiding that problem.

Singularity theories stress the oneness of God as a single ultimate bearer of properties, a sole metaphysical individual. On this sort of view, the three persons of the Trinity are not to be conceived as any sort of society or community of severally divine individuals or entities. The threeness which we have come to talk of as "persons" is rather to be understood as some less distinct internal relatedness within the life of the one God. As the greatest of singularity theorists, Augustine (A.D. 354-430), put it, Father, Son and Holy Spirit are themselves somehow just existent relations within the Godhead. In so categorizing the members of the Trinity, Augustine was drawing upon an ancient understanding of the status, or metaphysics, of relations, which is nowadays quite difficult for us to find at all plausible or even intelligible.

But Augustine offered some analogies to help us to grasp this view of the Trinity.[14] It was his view that the nature of God is mirrored in the nature of his creation, to the extent that even the tri-unity of the divine will be found reflected in creatures. He reminds us that God is referred to in the plural in an important passage in Genesis and is represented as saying: "Let *us* make man in *our* image" (Gen 1:26). So it is primarily to the life of human beings that we should look for analogies to help us understand the Trinity. Ideally, we need to find a triad of elements, the first of which begets the second, and the third of which binds the other two together, suggests Augustine. He offers such varied examples as: (1) an external object perceived, (2) the mind's representation of it, (3) the act of concentrating or focusing the mind on it; (1) the self as lover, (2) the object loved (which can be within that same self), (3) the love that binds; (1) the mind's memory *knowledge* of itself, (2) the mind's *understanding* of itself, (3) the mind's *will*, or love, of itself; and (1) the mind as remembering God, (2) the mind as knowing God, and (3) the mind as loving God.

But the most obvious problem with all these analogies is that they involve some sort of process or internal relatedness within the life of one person, and the doctrine of the Trinity is that, in some remotely plausible sense of "person," there are three persons which exist as the one God over all. Augustine thought that this, however, was about the best we can do. The Trinity is ultimately a mystery which we cannot hope to fathom fully, at least in this life.

Are these sorts of psychological analogies the best a singularity theory of the Trinity can manage? Well, Augustine and the many medieval philosophers who endorsed some form of singularity theory were typically pressured away from any recognition of a deeper diversity within the divine by their acceptance of a doctrine of divine simplicity, according to which there is no real ontological complexity or composition within the life of God. We have raised serious problems for such an idea in an earlier chapter. And it is difficult to see how anyone who endorses divine simplicity in the full-blown sense can accept even the analogies Augustine has given us as reflecting anything really to be found in the oneness of the divine. For these theorists, there can be no genuine ontological diversity, if strict simplicity really holds. Perhaps the best move for a singularity theorist who wants a plausible account of the Trinity, explicable by psychological analogies having to do with diversity within the sphere of individuality, is to jettison the constraints of the ancient doctrine of divine simplicity. When this is done, a new sort of analogy becomes available for the elaboration of a singularity theory.

Recall the two-minds view of God Incarnate developed in the previous section. Something like a multimind perspective could be used to explicate the doctrine of the Trinity as well. Suppose that there is only one ultimate divine bearer of properties, one fundamental individual who is God. If, as we argued in the previous section, it is compatible with the unity of the person of Christ that he have two minds, or two distinct spheres of mentality, then it should also be compatible with the unity of the one individual who is God that he have three divine minds, or three distinct spheres of perfect mentality, each capable of awareness and the initiation of action. And as the human mind of Christ was hierarchically answerable to the divine mind, imagine here a three-level hierarchy of answerability, with the mind designated as God the Father filling the role of overarching consciousness.

At this point the picture could be developed in different ways. Remembering that on any singularist theory, there is really only one divine individual, there is no conceptual pressure to assign each of the attributes constitutive of deity to each sphere of mentality within deity. Thus, it could be held that only the overarching consciousness of God the Father holds all the riches of omniscient knowledge. On this view, Christ need not have been speaking only of the limitations of his earthly mind when he talked of the passing away of heaven and earth and said: "But of that day or hour no one knows, not even the angels in heaven, nor the Son, but the Father alone" (Mk 13:32).

Likewise, it is possible for this sort of view to be developed in such a way that omnipotence is not assigned differentially to each sphere of mentality, thereby avoiding the coordination of activity problems of three omnipotent agents. The Son and the Spirit would then be divine, not in virtue of severally exemplifying all the attributes essential to deity, but rather through being centers of mentality belonging to the one true God as spheres of his own mindedness.

But there is nothing intrinsic to the multimind version of a singularity theory that would preclude our seeing each divine mind as enjoying the riches of omniscience and omnipotence. Each would be eternal, necessary components of the divine life. And each can be thought of as internally involved in contributing to the character and activities to be found in each of the others. The attribute of aseity, or ontological independence, could be reserved for the individual who exists with this multiminded richness of interior life, or could rather be attributed in qualified form to each of the spheres of mindedness. Neither Father, nor Son, nor Spirit depends for its existence on anything extratrinitarian, outside the life of divinity. But if there is ontologically only one ultimate divine entity, an individual God with these three spheres of mentality, it would be this single individual who most directly would answer to Anselm's concept of *the* greatest possible being and creation theology's concept of a single source of all.

Singularity theories seek to secure unambiguous monotheism, in line with the clear Judaic background of Christian theology. As such, there is much to be said for them. But it is difficult to render any confident judgment that any such theory can accommodate naturally the full data of biblical revelation and Christian experience. And it is a bit hard to see how any such theory will suffice to block what we have called the problem of the lonely God. Could I be said to experience the fullness of love just through my conscious mind's having a high regard for my unconscious mind, which in turn appreciated the conscious sphere? It is hard to see how even a richly differentiated self-love could suffice to capture all the facets that could possibly characterize the goodness of a full and perfect love. And if singularity theories are found inevitably wanting in this regard, it will be incumbent upon the Christian theist to find some form of a social theory to explicate the relation between threeness and oneness in the life of the triune God.

The main point that needs to be made here is that neither the doctrine of the Trinity nor the doctrine of the Incarnation is just an opaque mystery totally impenetrable to human thought. In each case we have seen that we can construct alternative, intelligible models or theories which offer quite interesting interpretations of initially paradoxical-looking ideas. As we have seen in the case of some of the attributes definitive of the divine, a fairly high degree of confidence concerning our conception of God at one level is compatible with having alternative explications, and thus with some degree of tentativeness, at a more fine-grained level of theological specificity. What is important to stress here, though, is that just as we can make progress in our efforts to think about the various basic attributes conceptually constitutive of our idea of deity, so, likewise, we can make important headway in our attempts to understand the most distinctive Christian claims about the greatest possible source of all.

Notes

Chapter 1: The Project of Philosophical Theology

[1] All pronominal references to God in this book will conform to traditional style without thereby necessarily conveying any commitment on the part of the author to any controversial social, political or theological theses or attitudes which might be associated in any way with that usage.

[2] Within the enterprise of philosophical theology we can explore such important religious ideas as those of original sin, atonement and sanctification, to give just a few examples.

[3] *Timaeus* 28d; Edith Hamilton and Huntington Cairns, eds., *Plato: The Collected Dialogues* (New York: Pantheon, 1961), p. 1162.

[4] Gregory Nazianzus, "The Second Theological Oration—On God," in *Christology of the Later Fathers*, ed. Edward R. Hardy (Philadelphia: The Westminster Press, 1954), p. 138.

[5] Gordon Kaufman, *God the Problem* (Cambridge: Harvard University Press, 1972), p. 95.

[6] A more modest version of this argument would end with the weaker conclusion "other things being equal, we have no reason to think that human concepts can apply to God." This more modest version will be no more of an obstacle to our procedures here than the version I examine. I leave the further exploration of this point to the reader.

[7] *Ontological* means something like "having to do with basic being or existence."

[8] For more on this, the reader might consult such books as E. L. Marshall, *Existence and Analogy* (London: Longmans, Green and Co., 1949); David Burrell, *Analogy and Philosophical Language* (New Haven: Yale University Press, 1973); and Janet Martin Soskice, *Metaphor and Religious Language* (Oxford: Oxford University Press, 1985).

[9] See Genesis 1:26-27.

Chapter 2: The Concept of God

[1] For an argument supporting the appropriateness of this, see William Charlton,

Philosophy and Christian Belief (London: Sheed and Ward, 1988).

[2]This sort of suggestion can be found in the work of the evangelical theologian J. I. Packer. See, for example, "What Do You Mean When You Say God?" *Christianity Today*, September 19, 1986, pp. 27-31.

[3]See S. N. Deane, trans., *St. Anselm: Basic Writings*, 2d ed. (LaSalle, Ill.: Open Court Publishing Company, 1968). More recently available is M. J. Charlesworth, trans., *St. Anselm's Proslogion* (Notre Dame: University of Notre Dame Press, 1979). Objections that can be raised against the Anselmian perspective are discussed at some length in Thomas V. Morris, *Anselmian Explorations* (Notre Dame: University of Notre Dame Press, 1987), especially in chapter one. This perspective is further developed and defended in George Schlesinger, *New Perspectives on Old-Time Religion* (Oxford: Oxford University Press, 1988).

[4]For more on this, see the editorial introduction to Thomas V. Morris, ed., *The Concept of God* (Oxford: Oxford University Press, 1987).

[5]Nicholas Wolterstorff, "Suffering Love," in *Philosophy and the Christian Faith*, ed. Thomas V. Morris (Notre Dame: University of Notre Dame Press, 1988), pp. 196-237.

[6]For an argument to this effect, see Thomas V. Morris, "A Theistic Proof of Perfection," *Sophia* 26 (July 1987):31-35.

Chapter 3: God's Goodness

[1]Boethius, *The Consolation of Philosophy*. See for example Arthur Hyman and James Walsh, eds., *Philosophy in the Middle Ages*, 2d ed. (Indianapolis: Hackett Publishing Company, 1983), p. 122.

[2]For an especially clear, straightforward discussion of the problem of evil, consult C. Stephen Evans, *Philosophy of Religion: Thinking about Faith* (Downers Grove: InterVarsity Press, 1985), pp. 130-40.

[3]See *Summa Contra Gentiles* 1.95.3.

[4]R. G. Swinburne, *The Coherence of Theism* (Oxford: Oxford University Press, 1977), pp. 146, 202. See also his book *The Existence of God* (Oxford: Oxford University Press, 1979), pp. 97-102.

[5]A *modal* conception or claim is, in this usage, one having to do with matters of possibility, impossibility or necessity.

[6]See Stephen Davis, *Logic and the Nature of God* (Grand Rapids: Eerdmans, 1983), chapter six, and Thomas V. Morris, *Anselmian Explorations* (Notre Dame: University of Notre Dame Press, 1987), chapter three.

Chapter 4: The Power of God

[1]Peter Geach, *Providence and Evil* (Cambridge: Cambridge University Press, 1977), p. 4.

²See, for example, Thomas P. Flint and Alfred J. Freddoso, "Maximal Power," in *The Existence and Nature of God,* ed. Alfred J. Freddoso (Notre Dame: University of Notre Dame Press, 1983), pp. 81-113; and Edward R. Wierenga, *The Nature of God: An Inquiry into Divine Attributes* (Ithaca, N.Y.: Cornell University Press, 1989), pp. 12-35.
³Anthony Kenny, *The God of the Philosophers* (Oxford: Oxford University Press, 1979), p. 96.
⁴Ibid.
⁵This is to be found in *Cur Deus Homo.* I have discussed it more fully in *Anselmian Explorations,* chapter four.
⁶Richard Creel, "Can God Know That He Is God?" *Religious Studies* 16 (June 1980):195-201.
⁷*Summa Contra Gentiles,* Anton C. Pegis, trans. (Notre Dame: University of Notre Dame Press, 1975), chapter 57.

Chapter 5: God's Knowledge
¹See, for example, Psalm 139.
²These phrases are to be pronounced "day dictoe" and "day ray." The former means, roughly, "concerning a proposition," the latter, "of a thing."
³Some philosophers have argued that knowledge *de re* ultimately can be reduced to knowledge *de dicto,* and so these are not after all two separate or distinct aspects of God's knowledge. From this point of view, my acquaintance with Paris yields extra knowledge only in the sense of providing me with additional true propositions about the city. Regardless of the outcome of this dispute, I have chosen to present the distinction here in order to help us clarify our grasp of the distinguishable facets of the divine knowledge.
⁴Some passages often cited in the New Testament are Mark 8:31; 9:31; 10:32-34; 14:13-15; 14:18-20; 14:27-30 (with all their parallels) and Matthew 17:27. Although these passages are indeed suggestive, none of them requires the idea of *complete* foreknowledge.
⁵For clear and detailed contemporary statements of the Molinist view, see the editor's introduction to Luis de Molina, *On Divine Foreknowledge,* ed. Alfred J. Freddoso (Ithaca, N.Y.: Cornell University Press, 1989) and Thomas P. Flint "Two Accounts of Providence," in *Divine and Human Action,* ed. Thomas V. Morris (Ithaca, N.Y.: Cornell University Press, 1988), pp. 147-81. For a critical perspective, see William Hasker, *God, Time, and Knowledge* (Ithaca, N.Y.: Cornell University Press, 1989).
⁶For a truly entertaining look at this issue from a different perspective, see J. L. Walls, "A Fable of Foreknowledge and Freedom," *Philosophy* 62 (January 1987):67-75.
⁷See Peter Geach, *Providence and Evil* (Cambridge: Cambridge University Press, 1977); George Schlesinger, *Religion and Scientific Method* (Dordrecht: D. Reidel Publishing Company, 1977); William Hasker (cited in note 5); and J. R. Lucas, *The Future*

(Oxford: Basil Blackwell, 1989).
[8]Lucas, *The Future*, p. 233.

Chapter 6: The Being of God
[1]We are here recapping and extending the distinctions made in chapter five.
[2]This reasoning also provides one basis for the famous ontological argument for the existence of God: The idea of God is that of a necessary being. If such a being is possible (i.e., existent in some possible world), it follows from his necessity that he exists in every possible world, and hence in the actual world. It is at least possible that there is a God. Thus, there is a God. It can be argued, however, that it is possible to incorporate into one's idea of God something like the property of necessary existence without endorsing any version of the ontological argument. To do this, for example, one could hold it to be required by the concept of God only that no individual could count as God unless that individual were such that if he existed in any possible world, he would exist in all possible worlds.
[3]Many theistic philosophers have also argued that a fully adequate explanatory account of our world requires the postulation of a necessarily existent Creator. This is the core of one famous version of the cosmological argument for the existence of God.
[4]J. N. Findlay, "Can God's Existence Be Disproved?" in *New Essays in Philosophical Theology*, ed. Antony Flew and Alasdair MacIntyre (New York: MacMillan, 1955), pp. 47-56.
[5]Pronounced "ah-say-ittee."
[6]For a clear review of some of these considerations, see William J. Wainwright, "God's Body," reprinted in *The Concept of God*, ed. Thomas V. Morris (Oxford: Oxford University Press, 1987), pp. 72-87.
[7]For some of these claims, see William E. Mann, "Simplicity and Immutability in God," reprinted in *The Concept of God*, ed. Thomas V. Morris (Oxford: Oxford University Press, 1987), pp. 253-267.
[8]See Eleonore Stump and Norman Kretzmann, "Absolute Simplicity," *Faith and Philosophy* 2 (October 1985):353-82.
[9]For a deft handling of some of the complexities here, see the essay by Stump and Kretzmann cited above, and the excellent rejoinder by William Hasker, "Simplicity and Freedom: A Response to Stump and Kretzmann," *Faith and Philosophy* 3 (April 1986):192-201.

Chapter 7: God's Eternity
[1]See the collection of texts edited by H. F. Stewart, E. K. Rand and S. J. Tester, *Boethius: The Theological Tractates and the Consolation of Philosophy* (London and Cambridge, Mass.: Harvard University Press, 1973), in particular *The Consolation of Philosophy*, book 5, prose 6 (422.5-424.31). This passage is discussed and amplified admirably in

Elenore Stump and Norman Kretzmann, "Eternity," reprinted in *The Concept of God*, ed. Thomas V. Morris (Oxford: Oxford University Press, 1987), pp. 219-52.

[2]See John K. Ryan, trans., *The Confessions of St. Augustine* (Garden City, N. J.: Image Books, 1960), p. 286. This is book two, chapter twelve of the original text.

[3]For more on this, see Richard Sorabji, *Time, Creation, and the Continuum* (Ithaca, N.Y.: Cornell University Press, 1983), chapter fourteen.

Chapter 8: The Creation

[1]Genesis 1:1.

[2]St. Thomas Aquinas, *Compendium of Theology*, trans. Cyril Vollert (St. Louis: B. Herder Book Company, 1948), p. 63 (chapter 68).

[3]Genesis 1:4, 10, 12, 18, 21, 25, 31.

[4]To illustrate the presence and absence of a natural principle of unity, consider a purported object consisting of one drawer of my desk, my Pelikan pen, my left foot, and Notre Dame's Golden Dome. This is clearly a "cooked up" entity for which there is no natural principle of unity. It is thus not to be considered a real individual composed of those named individuals. By way of contrast, there is a natural principle of unity according to which my desk drawer can be thought of legitimately as one entity.

[5]These propositions are stated for convenience in the past tense. Atemporalists will want to restate them tenselessly. It must be said, however, that it is a bit trickier to explain and justify these commitments from an atemporalist perspective since, on that view, there is no time before the creation of this world when God has real creative options, any one of which he can then go on to take. It should be noted also that I use the term 'universe' here to denote any created object or collection of such objects, whether physical or nonphysical, insofar as that object, or collection of objects, is all that exists distinct from God.

[6]For more on this, see Norman Kretzmann, "Goodness, Knowledge, and Indeterminacy in the Philosophy of Thomas Aquinas," *Journal of Philosophy*, supplement to vol. 80 (October 1983), pp. 631-49.

[7]Gottfried Wilhelm Leibniz, *Theodicy*, abridged ed., ed. Diogenes Allen, The Library of Liberal Arts (Indianapolis: Bobbs-Merrill, 1966), p. 35.

[8]Ibid., p. 101.

[9]Ibid., pp. 120-21.

[10]Ibid., p. 79.

[11]*Philosophical Review* 81 (July 1972):317-32, reprinted in *The Concept of God*, ed. Thomas V. Morris (Oxford: Oxford University Press, 1987) pp. 91-106.

[12]For more on this, see my *Anselmian Explorations*, chapter 9. See also Christopher Menzel, "Theism, Platonism, and the Metaphysics of Mathematics," *Faith and Philosophy* 4 (October 1987):365-82.

Chapter 9: God Incarnate and Triune

[1] Edward R. Hardy, ed., *Christology of the Later Fathers*, Library of Christian Classics (Philadelphia: Westminster Press, 1954), p. 373.

[2] More on the ancient Christian heresies can be found in such standard texts as Charles Gore, *The Incarnation of the Son of God* (London: John Murray, 1891); H. M. Relton, *A Study in Christology* (London: SPCK, 1917); E. G. Jay, *Son of Man, Son of God* (Montreal: McGill University Press, 1965); and J. N. D. Kelly, *Early Christian Doctrines*, rev. ed. (New York: Harper and Row, 1978). The heresy of psilanthropism is pronounced "sill-AN-throw-pizm" and comes from two Greek words meaning "mere man." Docetism is pronounced "DOE-seh-tizm."

[3] See Thomas V. Morris, *The Logic of God Incarnate* (Ithaca, N. Y.: Cornell University Press, 1986), for a full deployment of this strategy.

[4] For an example, see A. D. Smith, "God's Death," *Theology* 80 (July 1979):262-68.

[5] Hardy, *Christology of the Later Fathers*, pp. 363-364.

[6] Ibid., pp. 70-71.

[7] See *The Logic of God Incarnate*, pp. 102-7 and 149-62.

[8] For a popular presentation of this sort of view, see Robert Ornstein, *Multimind* (Boston: Houghton Mifflin, 1986).

[9] A clear presentation of the development of this doctrine, as well as the doctrine of the Incarnation, see J. N. D. Kelly, *Early Christian Doctrines*, rev. ed. (New York: Harper and Row, 1978). For the rejection of polytheism, see Cornelius Plantinga, Jr., "Social Trinity and Tritheism," in *Trinity, Incarnation and Atonement*, ed. Ronald J. Feenstra and Cornelius Plantinga, Jr. (Notre Dame: University of Notre Dame Press, 1989), pp. 21-47.

[10] Kelly, *Early Christian Doctrines*, p. 232.

[11] Richard Swinburne, "Could There Be More Than One God?" *Faith and Philosophy* 5 (July 1988):225-41.

[12] For an example of this sort of argument, and other related arguments, see William J. Wainwright, "Monotheism," in *Rationality, Religious Belief, and Moral Commitment*, ed. Robert Audi and William J. Wainwright (Ithaca, N. Y.: Cornell University Press, 1986), pp. 289-314.

[13] See, for example, John 5:37, 45; 6:57; 14:10; 15:10, and many other such passages in the Gospels.

[14] For a convenient summary and references, see Kelly, *Early Christian Doctrines*, pp. 271-79.

Books for Further Reading

Alston, William P. *Divine Nature and Human Language*. Ithaca, N. Y.: Cornell University Press, 1989.

Brody, Baruch. *Readings in the Philosophy of Religion: An Analytic Approach*. Englewood Cliffs, N. J.: Prentice-Hall, 1974.

Brown, David. *The Divine Trinity*. LaSalle, Ill.: Open Court Publishing Company, 1985.

Cahn, S., and Shatz, D., eds. *Contemporary Philosophy of Religion*. Oxford: Oxford University Press, 1982.

Creel, Richard E. *Divine Impassibility*. Cambridge: Cambridge University Press, 1985.

Davis, Stephen. *Logic and the Nature of God*. Grand Rapids: Eerdmans, 1983.

Dore, Clement. *Theism*. Dordrecht: D. Reidel Publishing Company, 1984.

Durrant, Michael. *The Logical Status of 'God.'* London: St. Martin's Press, 1973.

———. *Theology and Intelligibility*. London: Routledge and Kegan Paul, 1973.

Feenstra, Ronald J., and Plantinga, Cornelius Jr., eds. *Trinity, Incarnation, and Atonement: Philosophical and Theological Essays*. Notre Dame: University of Notre Dame Press, 1989.

Freddoso, Alfred J., ed. *The Existence and Nature of God*. Notre Dame: University of Notre Dame Press, 1983.

———, trans. *Luis de Molina: On Divine Foreknowledge*. Ithaca, N. Y.: Cornell University Press, 1988.

Geach, Peter. *Providence and Evil*. Cambridge: Cambridge University Press, 1977.

Hasker, William. *God, Time and Knowledge*. Ithaca, N. Y.: Cornell University Press, 1989.

Helm, Paul. *Divine Commands and Morality*. Oxford: Oxford University Press, 1981.

———. *Eternal God*. Oxford: Oxford University Press, 1988.

Jantzen, Grace. *God's World, God's Body*. Philadelphia: Westminster Press, 1984.

Kenny, Anthony. *The God of the Philosophers*. Oxford: Oxford University Press, 1979.

Kvanvig, Jonathan. *The Possibility of an All-Knowing God*. London: MacMillan Press, 1986.

Morris, Thomas V. *Anselmian Explorations.* Notre Dame: University of Notre Dame Press, 1987.

———. *The Concept of God.* Oxford: Oxford University Press, 1987.

———. *The Logic of God Incarnate.* Ithaca, N.Y.: Cornell University Press, 1986.

———, ed. *Divine and Human Action: Essays in the Metaphysics of Theism.* Ithaca, N.Y.: Cornell University Press, 1988.

———, ed. *Philosophy and the Christian Faith.* Notre Dame: University of Notre Dame Press, 1988.

Pike, Nelson. *God and Timelessness.* New York: Schocken Press, 1970.

Plantinga, Alvin. *Does God Have a Nature?* Milwaukee: Marquette University Press, 1980.

Ross, J. *Philosophical Theology.* 2d ed. Indianapolis: Bobbs-Merrill, 1980.

Schlesinger, George. *New Perspectives on Old-Time Religion.* Oxford: Oxford University Press, 1988.

Swinburne, Richard. *The Coherence of Theism.* Oxford: Oxford University Press, 1977.

Urban, L., and Walton, D., eds. *The Power of God: Readings on Omnipotence and Evil.* Oxford: Oxford University Press, 1978.

Ward, Keith. *Rational Theology and the Creativity of God.* Oxford: Basil Blackwell, 1982.

Wierenga, Edward R. *The Nature of God: An Inquiry into Divine Attributes.* Ithaca, N. Y.: Cornell University Press, 1989.